THE SOUND OF ONLY

Rev. Eric N. Betts

Table of Contents

PROLOGUE 1
- Revelation 1:3..1

THE SILENCE BEFORE THE SOUND.................................9
- Revelation 8:1..9

AWAKENING OF SURRENDER 20
- Luke 9:23 20

RESTORING OUR SANITY 40
- Isaiah 26:3...40

Sanity List..54

Things that make me crazy:..54

Things I actually have control over:...........................54

SURRENDERING OUR LIVES TO GOD 64
- Proverbs 3:5,6..64

MIRROR TO THE SOUL...81
- James 1:23-25...81

BEARING THE FAULT.. 100
- Psalms 51:17.. 100

ASHES OF PRIDE 111
- Psalms 139:23-24.. 111

HOLLOW PRAYERS..126
- Proverbs 28:13 126

SEEKING RESTORATION 136
- Isaiah 43:1..136

MAKING AMENDS - UNFINISHED BUSINESS.....................156
- Matthew 5:23-24...156

DAILY RECKONING AND SURRENDER......................173

- 1 Corinthians 15:31 173

THE POWER OF "ONLY": A SINGLE PRAYER THAT CHANGES EVERYTHING. 192

THE ROMANS ROAD 207
- Revelation 22:20,21 207

PROLOGUE

"Blessed is the one who reads aloud the words of this prophecy, and blessed are those who hear it and take to heart what is written in it, because the time is near."
- Revelation 1:3

The ultimate invitation is running out. Not in the abstract way we usually mean when we say those words. Not in the way you might warn someone late for an appointment, or urge a friend to finally pursue their dreams. This invitation is literal. Final. Absolute. Time is running out.

And yet, we live as if we have endless amounts of it. We schedule our lives in five-year plans. We save for retirement. We tell ourselves there will always be a tomorrow. Tomorrow, we'll get right with God. Tomorrow, we'll surrender what we've been holding back.

But what if there is no tomorrow? What if the very fabric of time, the thing we treated as infinite, as guaranteed, is about to collapse? What if the next sound you hear isn't your alarm clock, or your phone notification, or the hum of traffic outside your window, but something far older, far more terrible, far more final? The sound of a trumpet.

Welcome to *The Sound of ONLY.*

My name may be on the cover, but make no mistake: I am not your teacher. I am not your guru. I am not perched on some spiritual mountaintop, looking down with judgment or pity. I am standing beside you in the valley, looking up at the same mountain, feeling the same trembling in my soul that you might be feeling right now.

This is not a book of answers. It is a book of questions. Hard questions. The kind we spend our entire lives avoiding, because we already know what they'll reveal, if we are honest enough to ask them.

The central question of this series is devastatingly simple: Are you truly ready to be lifted? Not, do you go to church?, do you know the right verses? Have you said the right prayer at the right altar at the right moment? But: Are you ready? Is your soul prepared? Is your will surrendered?

When the trumpet sounds, when the sky tears open, when the voice of the Almighty splits the heavens, will you rise, or will you remain?

Before we go any further, you must understand something. This book will not comfort you. If you came searching for gentle reassurance or if you hoped for soft platitudes about God's love and grace, you have come to the wrong place. Though His love is real and His grace is infinite, grace is not a blanket we pull over our heads when the world feels too heavy. Grace is not sedation for the soul; grace is a force.

It does not soothe…it *shapes*. It does not excuse…it *exposes*. It does not leave us unchanged; it demands something of us. It drags us, often unwillingly, into truths that are inconvenient, uncomfortable, and impossible to ignore.

The world we inhabit runs on two great illusions. They are so deeply embedded in our thinking that we no longer recognize them as illusions at all. They have become the water we swim in, the air we breathe, silent assumptions shaping every choice we make.

The first illusion is the illusion of control. We make plans. We set goals. We build careers and families and retirement funds. We install security systems, buy insurance policies, and check the weather forecast before stepping outside. We operate under the unspoken assumption that if we are smart enough, careful enough, prepared enough… we can manage the outcomes of our lives.

This is a lie.

The second illusion is the illusion of time. We treat time as though it were infinite currency, something we can spend casually because tomorrow will refill the account. We say things like, *I'll deal with that later,* or *I'll get serious about my faith when I'm older,* or *There's plenty of time to make things right.*

So, we postpone the hard conversations, avoid the necessary surrenders, and delay the painful admissions of fault, convincing ourselves that we will become braver, wiser versions of ourselves in some undefined future. We tell ourselves that tomorrow will give us the courage we lack today, that time will soften the truths we are unwilling to face, that regret can be rescheduled. But the future is not a warehouse stocked with opportunities; it is a narrowing door, and we are running out of hallway even as we pretend the corridor is endless.

We tell ourselves we will become braver versions of ourselves in the future, more honest, more faithful, more awake. But the future is not a warehouse stocked with opportunities; it is a narrowing door, and we are running out of hallway even as we pretend the corridor is endless. We believe, truly believe, that time is on our side. This, too, is a lie, because time is not our ally. It is a silent eraser, removing possibilities one heartbeat at a time. It does not announce its thefts; it simply leaves us with what remains.

And the events that are about to unfold in this book, beginning with a city gone dark and ending with the unmistakable blast of a trumpet, will shatter both of these illusions completely and irrevocably. Control will collapse, time will betray us, and what will be left is not comfort. It will be true.

Let me be clear about something else. This is not a book about scaring you into heaven. Fear *is* a useful emotion—it alerts us to danger, sharpens our senses, jolts us awake when we drift too close to the edge. But fear alone cannot save you. Fear will not carry you when the moment comes, when the ground gives way beneath your certainties, and all the rehearsed answers fall silent.

What this book offers is something far more powerful and far more demanding than fear. It offers clarity. It offers truth. It offers the kind of brutal, uncompromising honesty that strips away every excuse, every religious performance, every comfortable self-deception we have been hiding behind for years.

I have sat in churches my entire life. I have heard thousands of sermons, sung thousands of worship songs, whispered countless prayers. I have read my Bible, served on committees, volunteered at events, raised my hands at the right moments, and bowed my head at the right ones. Somewhere along the way, I became very, very good at looking the part. I knew the language. I knew the posture. I knew exactly what to say and when to say it.

But knowing the lines of a play does not make you the character... and reciting the words of faith does not make you faithful.

There came a moment in my life, a moment I will share with you as we journey through these chapters, when I realized, with a kind of quiet horror that hollowed me out from the inside, that I had built an entire religious life that had almost nothing to do with actual surrender to God.

I had constructed an elaborate stage set that looked like devotion, sounded like commitment, felt like righteousness. From the outside, it was flawless. From the inside, it was empty. It was not worship at all, but another expression of my own will, my own control, my own carefully guarded agenda. I was not offering my life to God; I was negotiating with Him. I was not trusting Him; I was managing Him.

I had turned faith into a system I could operate, a performance I could perfect, a mask I could wear so convincingly that even I forgot it was a mask. And in doing so, I insulated myself from the one thing I claimed to desire most: surrender.

By the time I finally saw it, I was already standing on the edge of something I could not out-organize, out-pray, or out-plan. I was using God rather than yielding to Him. I was controlling my faith rather than living it.

And I was completely, utterly unprepared for what was coming.

Maybe you're different. Perhaps you really are one of the rare souls who has laid down your will, who lives in constant surrender, who wakes each morning with nothing in your hands and nothing on your agenda except whatever God wants from you that day. And if, as you read those words, you can say without hesitation that they truly describe your life, then you probably don't need this book.

But I suspect that's not you. I suspect that if you're still listening to these words, it's because something inside you already knows, has known for a while, that there is a gap between the faith you profess and the life you actually live. There is a disconnect between the person you present at church and the person you are at three in the morning when you cannot sleep. There is a question you have been avoiding, a surrender you have been postponing, a truth you have been running from.

And time is running out.

The format of this series is intentional. Over the next chapters, I will take you on a spiritual journey that mirrors the 12 steps of recovery programs, but viewed through the lens of preparing for the rapture. Why the 12 steps? Because in all my searching, I've found them to be the most honest, the most practical framework for true surrender. They don't sugarcoat anything, and they don't pretend we have it all together. That's exactly why I'm sharing them with you, because this journey is about facing the truth, not pretending, and I want to give you a roadmap that actually works.

They don't let you hide behind theology. They don't let you substitute religious activity for real transformation. They demand a thorough inventory of your heart. They require honest admission of your faults and failures. They force you to look at yourself with unflinching clarity, to see the parts of yourself you've been avoiding, and then take concrete action to change. There are no shortcuts, no illusions, no pretending you're further along than you really are. And that is exactly what this moment in history requires of us.

Each chapter will tell a story. Some of these stories are drawn from real events. Some are composites of experiences I've witnessed or lived. Some are parables crafted to illuminate a truth that might otherwise remain hidden. But every single one of them points to the same undeniable reality: the trumpet is about to sound, and the only question that truly matters is whether you are ready to answer its call.

But I need to warn you about something. This journey will cost you. It will strip away your illusions, shatter your excuses, and dismantle the carefully curated image you've spent years projecting. It will challenge the comfortable, predictable performance of faith that asks nothing of you and demands no real change. Most of all, it will cost you your will, and that is the one thing most of us cling to with everything we have, the one thing we guard more fiercely than anything else.

We are quick to surrender the surface-level things. We will give our time, our money, our Sunday mornings, and our Wednesday evenings. We will surrender the sins that society tells us are unacceptable. We will try to surrender the bad habits, the petty complaints, the visible faults that make us look like we are making progress. But the heart of who we are, the place where every ultimate choice is made, the seat of our will, we protect it. We disguise it, justify it, and hide it even from ourselves.

And yet, that is exactly what this journey calls for. It asks for nothing less than a full surrender of the self we think we own, the life we think we control, the choices we cling to as if they define us. Because until we relinquish our will, we have not truly begun.

And that is exactly what God is coming for. Not your money. Not your time. Not your talent, your service, or your religious activity. He is coming for your will, the last hidden place where *you* still sit on the throne, the final stronghold of your pride and self-rule. He is coming to tear down that throne, to strip away everything you have clung to, everything you have convinced yourself defines you, so that what remains is not the version of yourself you have built, but the version He created you to be.

In our modern, therapeutic version of Christianity, we rarely talk about God running out of patience. We prefer to dwell on His infinite love, His boundless mercy, His eternal grace. And yes, all of that is true, absolutely true. But it is not the whole truth.

The whole truth is that God has given humanity chance after chance, after chance. He has sent prophets and preachers, signs and wonders. He has whispered in still, small voices and shouted through storms and catastrophes. He has been patient beyond all human understanding, waiting for us to turn, to repent, to surrender. And yet, even patience has a boundary. Even grace has its final hour.

There is a limit. There is a last call. And when that trumpet sounds, when that final, thunderous blast tears through the fabric of reality, there will be no more chances. No more negotiations. No more time to weigh comfort against obedience. The moment for decision will have passed. The door will have closed. And then, in that absolute, unalterable instant, you will either rise to meet Him, fully surrendered, fully alive, or you will remain behind, forced to face the consequences of every choice you postponed, every act of compromise, every corner of your heart you refused to yield.

This is not a distant story. It is not a metaphor. It is a call, a fierce, unrelenting call, and it will not wait for you to be ready. The question is not whether you *want* to answer. The question is whether you will.

I cannot tell you when that moment will come. No one can. Jesus Himself said that no one knows the day or the hour, not even the angels in heaven. But what I *can* tell you, what I *must* tell you, is that everything around us is pointing in the same direction. The world is unraveling. The systems we trusted are failing. The institutions we leaned on are cracking. The moral foundations we built our lives upon are eroding. Chaos is rising. Darkness is spreading.

This book will dismantle every excuse and every comfortable lie we tell ourselves about our spiritual condition. We will move beyond religious performance into what real surrender looks like in daily, concrete practice. This will not be easy. There will be moments when you want to stop reading, when the mirror these pages hold up reflects something you would rather not see. When that happens, lean in instead of pulling away, because that resistance is not wisdom; it is your will fighting to stay in control.

So, I ask you, not as a preacher, not as a writer, but as someone who has stood where you are now, are you ready? Not *theoretically* ready. Not "I hope so" ready. Not "I think I've done enough" ready.

But ready in the secret place of your soul, in the space only you and God can see.

When that trumpet finally sounds, when the sky breaks open, and the voice of the Almighty calls His children home, the only thing that will matter is whether you belong to Him completely, not partially, not in intention, but without reservation.

That completeness, that total surrender, is what this book is about. So ask yourself, *am I truly ready to be lifted?*

CHAPTER 1:
THE SILENCE BEFORE THE SOUND

"When He opened the seventh seal, there was silence in heaven for about half an hour."
- Revelation 8:1

Michael Flowers had not prayed in seven years, and he could pinpoint the exact moment prayer left his body. It was February third, a Tuesday, in a hospital waiting room that smelled like disinfectant and false hope. The doctor stood in front of him with fingers laced together, eyes that refused to settle on Michael's face, and a voice that had clearly been practiced this speech far too many times.

Stage four. Inoperable. Six months, maybe less. Each word fell like dirt onto a grave that had not yet been dug, and Michael remembered thinking that grief should be louder, more violent, but instead it moved through him like cold water, seeping into places he didn't know could hurt.

Sarah squeezed his hand that day and whispered that everything was going to be okay. She always said that, even when there was no evidence left in the world to support it. She said it with the same calm faith she had carried her entire life, the faith that woke her before sunrise to give thanks, that bowed her head over every meal, that believed miracles were not rare accidents but daily occurrences if you were good enough, faithful enough, devoted enough. Sarah had done everything right. She had prayed when life was easy and when it was cruel. She believed with the kind of certainty Michael had never been able to match.

She was gone in four months. Four months of watching her body betray her, of pretending not to notice how her wedding ring slipped off fingers that had once clung to his in the dark. Four months of begging a God he was beginning not to recognize for anything at all, time, mercy, even pain if it meant she could stay. But nothing came. When Sarah finally stopped breathing, something inside Michael tore open and stayed that way. Not rage, not even anger, just an endless hollow where faith used to live.

That was the moment he stopped praying. There was no dramatic outburst, no shaking fist at the ceiling. Only the quiet, irreversible closing of a door. If this was how God rewarded the woman who had loved Him her entire life, then God could have His religion back. Michael wanted no part of it. All that remained was the ache, the unbearable weight of waking each morning in a world where Sarah no longer existed.

That was seven years ago. Now Michael stood at the window of his tenth-floor apartment in downtown Chicago, staring out at a city that had been swallowed by darkness for three days. Not just the kind of darkness caused by a power outage, where emergency lights flicker, and alarms beep in uneasy reassurance. No. This was darkness that seemed deliberate, almost conscious, a void that pressed down on the city as though it were punishing it. It had begun on Monday morning, not gradually, block by block, but all at once. One moment, the city had been alive with lights, engines, voices, the endless pulse of life, and the next, everything had stopped. Every light extinguished. Every screen is dead.

On that first day, people had been annoyed and frustrated. It was the kind of irritation born of inconvenience, of disrupted plans, of the arrogance of assuming that the world owed them normalcy. They had spilled into the streets, waving dead phones, theorizing endlessly: solar flares, EMPs, terrorist attacks, the predictions growing ever more absurd with each passing hour. By the second day, Illinois had curdled into a state of anxious hysteria. Without information, without the hum of human life, the city itself seemed to shrink inward, suffocating beneath its own emptiness. The silence of the streets felt alive, oppressive, like something unseen was holding its breath.

And now it was the third day, Thursday, or at least what Michael thought must be Thursday. Without clocks, without screens, without the markers of ordinary time, he had begun to count sunrises. Three. Three sunrises had passed since the city went dark, and now the stillness had shifted from anxious waiting to something else, something deeper, something that clawed at the marrow of his mind. At the same time, he had tossed and turned on his couch through the long hours of the night, unable to sleep, unable to silence the endless permutations of "what if" and "how," the city had become more than quiet.

Even in the darkness, humans are noisy creatures, filling empty spaces with sound to assert that they exist. But the city no longer made noise. It was holding its breath, and as Michael pressed his forehead against the cold glass of the window, he realized with a jolt that he could hear nothing but the obscene sound of his own breathing.

Michael had prepared for disasters before. After Sarah died, after he had walked away from faith in God, from the church, from any divine power that seemed to betray those who loved Him most, he had become something of a survivalist. Not the extreme kind, no, but practical, rational, meticulous. Water, canned food, candles, matches, a hand-crank radio, first aid supplies, all the tools for a predictable catastrophe. He could survive storms, social unrest, economic collapse, and even earthquakes. But not this. Not this darkness that pressed against the bones of the city and against the soul. This was silence with weight, with a presence that did not belong to any rational world he knew. It was a judgment of a different sort, one that no checklist could prepare for, no manual could instruct against.

He shook his head, trying to dislodge the creeping thought. That was the old programming speaking, the sermons, the Sunday school lessons, the warnings about judgment, and the end times. But he had thought he was done with all of it. For seven years, he had lived believing he could divorce himself from faith the way one signs papers and divides assets: clean, permanent, resolved. And yet, standing here on the third day of a city swallowed whole by darkness, he felt it again. Not faith, not exactly, but the ghost of it. A phantom limb he had believed amputated long ago, aching and absent and yet impossible to ignore.

Memories crept unbidden: the end-of-times stories from Sunday school, Sarah's earnest eyes in the back pew, Revelation's seven seals and seven trumpets, the silence in heaven for half an hour, a detail he had once dismissed as absurd now gnawed at him with unbearable relevance. He shook his head violently, as if the motion could dislodge the thought entirely. But the silence outside, the oppressive waiting, refused to let go. It was a void that demanded recognition. It was a mirror, reflecting the emptiness he had carried within him ever since God had failed Sarah. It was a blackout, yes, but also a testament, a cruel reflection of a world stripped bare, devoid not just of light but of mercy, of presence, of the assurance he had once sought in prayers now long abandoned.

It was just a blackout. Impossible, comprehensive, but still just a blackout. There had to be a rational explanation. There always was. Michael moved through his apartment by candlelight, checking the supplies again, not because he doubted their presence, but because the act itself gave him something to hold onto. Water: three cases, twenty-four bottles each. Food: enough for two weeks if rationed carefully. Candles: running low; he would need to conserve. First aid kit: untouched. Radio: silent, useless, yet he kept it close, as if the crackle of another human voice might remind him that the world outside still followed rules he could understand. He wasn't alone. Millions of people were out there somewhere, checking their own inventories, grappling with the same uncertainty. He told himself this over and over. Logical. Predictable. Controllable. And yet the stillness pressed against him, unyielding, heavier than grief, heavier than anything he had known since Sarah died. This was different. Vast. Quiet that wasn't quiet. And still he clung to routine, to counting and checking, because to acknowledge the possibility that there was no explanation, no order, was something he could not yet face.

What if Sarah had been right? What if all those years of faithful prayer, of Bible reading, of unwavering belief, had not been wasted? What if the reason she faced death with such unshakable peace wasn't denial or delusion, but something real? Something true? Something that had held her steady in the face of the impossible? And what if he had been wrong all along?

The thought struck him like a blow. His hands clenched into fists, nails digging into palms he couldn't feel, heart hammering. The silence around him, the blackout, the stillness of the city, the absence of all sound and light, suddenly felt like it was holding its breath, waiting for an answer he could not give. The silence that existed before God spoke creation into being. Could this darkness, this impossible suspension of everything that made modern life function, be more than chaos? Could it be an announcement?

He stood abruptly, turning away from the window, angry at himself, angry at the memory of Sarah, angry at the stubbornness of his own mind. This thinking was useless. Dangerous. Human minds were wired to grasp for meaning, to demand patterns, to divine gods in the misfortunes that plagued them. He could feel himself sliding into the trap, the same trap countless humans had fallen into for millennia, the trap of trying to explain every catastrophe as divine will. But he had rejected that. He had lived seven years beyond it. And yet... the thought persisted, clawing its way back, insistent, irritating, maddening.

Michael's chest tightened. The rational part of him screamed, *Stop. This is useless. This is nonsense.* But another part, the part that remembered her face, her certainty, her peace, refused to be silenced. It whispered in a voice he hadn't heard in years, a voice he had tried to bury: *What if she was right?*

And he hated it. Hated himself for letting it in. Hated the faint, gnawing possibility that faith, something he had sworn off forever, might still exist.

He walked back to the window, desperate to anchor himself in some semblance of reality. And then it happened, the silence deepened. He didn't know how that was possible. The silence had already been absolute, yet now it penetrated him in a way that bypassed his ears entirely, sinking straight into his chest, into his bones, into the very core of his being. It became more than emptiness. It became present. It became judgment. It became the silence of eternity, the silence that preceded creation itself.

Michael's heart hammered in his ribs, a frantic drum against the infinite quiet. He pressed both hands to the glass, clutching for something solid, something real, something human. And then it came.

A trumpet.

Not a trumpet that any human could have produced. Not the brassy cry of a jazz band in a Chicago club, not a school marching band, not a street performer. This sound had no origin that could be measured, no source that could exist within the natural world. It was everywhere and nowhere at once. It came from above, from beneath, from the marrow of his bones, and from some place beyond him. The note was singular, eternal, unwavering, impossibly pure. It was not music. It was authority made audible. It was power incarnate. The universe itself seemed to bow beneath it.

His hands slipped from the glass. His knees buckled. He sank to the floor, back against the wall, pressing his hands to his ears though he knew it could not be blocked. The sound was not entering through his ears. It was entering through him, through the soul he had thought long dead, the faith he had locked away seven years ago. The trumpet continued, unrelenting, and time fractured. Seconds became immeasurable. Minutes lost all meaning. There was only the note, filling every particle of space, commanding reality, demanding recognition. And then, just as suddenly as it began, it ended.

The silence that followed was different. It was not waiting this time. It was a consequence. It was the echo of divine authority reverberating through the world, the sound of existence realizing something had shifted irreversibly. Michael remained on the floor, body trembling, breath ragged, mind reeling between denial, incredulity, and the stark, awful certainty of what he had experienced.

It could not be. It defied every law, every understanding, every rational framework he had ever trusted. And yet he had heard it. Not merely heard it, but felt it in his chest, in his soul, in the place where faith had been exiled, abandoned, and sealed away. The trumpet, the first, or perhaps the last, had sounded.

Memories from childhood flooded him: sermons about death, judgment, the end of days, the seven seals, the seven trumpets, the seven bowls. He had never cared to memorize the order, too absorbed in his own cleverness, too committed to the idea that it was all metaphor, all human attempts to impose meaning on chaos. But the sound that had just struck the world was no metaphor. This was divine. This was absolute. This was God's voice, commanding attention, demanding acknowledgment, rewriting everything in its presence.

He forced himself to stand, legs trembling like liquid, hands braced on the wall for support. He returned to the window, part of him wanting to close his eyes, to pretend he had imagined it. Below, the streets remained empty. Silent. But as his vision sharpened, he saw what the trumpet had revealed: piles of clothes scattered across sidewalks and crosswalks, arranged as if the wearers had simply vanished, leaving only the echo of human form behind.

The piles kept coming. Jackets, shirts, pants, shoes, arranged as if the people who had worn them had simply vanished into thin air. One pile. Another. More, too many to count, scattered across the street like remnants of a world that had ceased to exist. Michael's hands shook so violently he had to clutch the windowsill, as if holding on could anchor him to reason, to reality, to sanity. His breath fogged the glass, and his mind churned in frantic denial, grasping for explanations: hallucination, trick of the light, mass panic. Scientific reasoning. Rational thought. Anything that would let him ignore the truth clawing at the edges of his understanding.

But his soul, that part of him he had tried to kill seven years ago, screamed a different language. The part that had listened to Sarah pray every night, the part that remembered what it felt like to believe in something larger than himself, that part was screaming now: *You missed it. You weren't ready. You were left behind.*

No. That was insane. Fevered. Impossible. People didn't just vanish, leaving clothes behind in the streets like discarded shadows. That's not how the universe worked. Not reality. Not nature. And yet... the city had been dark for three days. Every piece of modern technology is frozen. He had heard a sound no human could produce. And now, the streets were littered with the remnants of human life, empty vessels where living beings should have been. Except it wasn't "except" anymore. It was true. Undeniable, inescapable truth.

Michael sank to his knees, this time not from shock, but from the full, awful weight of understanding. The realization hit him like a storm, tearing through every rational thought he had clung to for years. Sarah had been right. All those prayers he had mocked, all the hope he had dismissed, all the faith he had derided, they had been real. True. And he had walked away. Deliberately. With arrogance, with pride, with a certainty so absolute it had blinded him. He had let grief become his God, anger become his truth, and pride become his prison. And now...the trumpet had sounded, and he was still here.

The storm crashed over him, relentless. Not just that he had been wrong, but that he had *seven years*. Seven years to reconsider. Seven years to humble himself, to admit that maybe the God he blamed for Sarah's death had a perspective he could not see, a plan he could not understand. Seven years wasted.

He thought of her final weeks. Her body failing, her voice soft but unwavering, trying to warn him, to prepare him, to talk of being ready, of making sure he was right with God. And he had shut her down. First gently, then with irritation, then finally with anger. "I don't want to hear it," he had said. "If God is real and good, He wouldn't be taking you." He had believed himself clever. Certain. Unassailable. And she had looked at him with such sadness, not judgment, not anger, just sorrow, as if she could see the future and knew he was choosing a path that would cost him everything.

Now, lying against the hardwood floor, shoulder shaking, tears burning, Michael understood the full, crushing consequence of that choice. Seven years of stubborn pride had brought him here. The trumpet had sounded, the faithful had been taken, and he had refused. He was left. Left physically, spiritually, irreversibly. The weight of it pressed down on him harder than grief ever had. He pressed his forehead to the floor, gasping, the words trapped in his throat: *I'm sorry. I'm sorry, Sarah. I'm sorry, God. I was too proud. Too certain. Too blind.*

But it was too late. Sorry could not change what had already happened. Sorry, could not undo seven years of willful rejection, seven years of walking away from the one truth that had been steadfast, waiting, patient. Sorry could not prepare him for whatever came next. He was here. Alone. Left behind.

And the door had closed.

Michael Flowers, who had not prayed in seven years, found himself on his knees in the middle of his dark apartment. Not the polite, practiced prayers of childhood, not the memorized lines from church services, but something raw tore out of him, something feral and broken and afraid. His palms were flat against the hardwood floor, his forehead bowed so low it nearly touched the boards, his shoulders trembling as if his body no longer knew how to hold itself together.

"God… God, please," he whispered, his voice cracking, the word feeling foreign in his mouth. "I don't even know how to talk to you anymore. I don't remember how to do this right. I don't know the words. I don't deserve the words."

His throat closed, a sob ripping through him so violently he had to gasp for air. Tears spilled onto the floor, blurring the dark shapes of the room until all he could see was the warped reflection of himself in grief. "If you're listening… if there's any mercy left anywhere in this world… I'm sorry. I was wrong about everything. I was so angry, so sure my pain meant you didn't care. I told myself I was smarter than faith, stronger without it. But I see now. God, I see what I did. I see what I turned away from."

His hands curled into fists, knuckles white, nails digging into the wood as if he could hold the moment still. "Please," he said again, louder now, voice breaking apart. "Please don't let this be the end.

Please don't let me be left like this. I don't want to be alone anymore. I don't want to be right, I just want to be forgiven. I'll do anything. Anything. I surrender. You win. I was wrong, and you were right, and I don't care about pride or logic or being clever anymore. I just want you."

The words tumbled out of him in gasps and sobs, some spoken, some barely sounding at all, just breath and grief and the ache of seven wasted years breaking loose inside his chest. His body folded in on itself, spine curved, face pressed to the floor as if he were trying to disappear into the wood beneath him. Fear wrapped around his heart like a vise, the terror of being too late, of begging at a door already closed, of finally understanding what he had thrown away.

"I'm scared," he whispered, the honesty of it shattering him. "I don't know what comes next. I don't know how to survive this. Please, God, don't leave me here."

And there, kneeling in the dark, shaking, soaked in tears, with nothing left but desperation, Michael prayed, not because he believed he deserved an answer, but because hopelessness had stripped him bare, and prayer was all he had left.

Before we move forward in this journey of accountability and surrender, I need you to sit with Michael's story for a moment, not as a character in a narrative, but as a mirror. How many years has it been since you truly prayed, not performed, not recited, but prayed with desperation and honesty? How long have you been saying no to God while telling yourself it isn't really no, just not yet, just not now, just give me a little more time? And how certain are you that there will be a tomorrow? Michael thought he had time. He believed it with the quiet arrogance of someone who assumes the door will always remain open, and he spent seven long years clinging to his anger, his grief, his pride, wasting days he thought he owned.

So, how much time do you have? How much time do any of us have? The trumpet that Michael heard in Chicago is not confined to his story; it is coming for us all. Maybe not today. Maybe not tomorrow. But soon. Sooner than we think, sooner than we are prepared for. And when it sounds, the only question that will matter is the one we have been circling from the very beginning: are you ready? Not ready in theory, not ready on paper, but ready in the core of your being, ready in your will, ready in the hidden place where you have been calling resistance wisdom. Michael was not ready, and it cost him everything. Do not let his story become your own. Do not wait until the trumpet sounds to admit you were wrong. Do not wait until darkness falls to wish you had surrendered in the light.

CHAPTER 2:
AWAKENING OF SURRENDER

"Then he said to them all: Whoever wants to be my disciple must deny themselves and take up their cross daily and follow me."
- **Luke 9:23**

Abraham hated his name. He hated it since the third grade, when Miss Henderson had stood at the front of the classroom and taught the kids about the biblical Abraham. Every child had turned to look at him with that mix of amusement and pity reserved for children whose parents had saddled them with expectations they couldn't possibly meet. Abraham. The father of faith. The friend of God. The man who had been willing to sacrifice his own son because God asked him to. How do you live up to that? You don't. That was the answer Abraham had arrived at by the time he was thirty-five years old, successful by every metric society revered, and utterly bankrupt in every way that truly mattered.

He was a partner at one of Chicago's most prestigious law firms. His name was on the letterhead. He had the corner office with a view of Lake Michigan. A luxury condo in Lincoln Park, a BMW in the parking lot, suits in his closet like soldiers at attention. Season tickets to the Bulls and the symphony, though he rarely used them. A network of contacts that could open any door, a reputation that preceded him into every boardroom, a bank account that would have seemed like fantasy money to his parents, who had worked two jobs just to keep the lights on while he was growing up. He had everything.

And it was killing him. Not metaphorically. Not in that vague, polished way successful people sometimes claim when they want sympathy for having too much. Abraham was literally dying. Every day, his body betrayed him a little more, a constant reminder that no amount of money or prestige could buy immunity. His heart didn't just race, it skipped, thudded, and faltered as if it were warning him in Morse code. The hypertension had him on edge, nerves raw and frayed, while the arrhythmia made every breath a gamble. Simple things, climbing the stairs to his condo, bending over to tie his shoes, left him dizzy, chest tight, like he was carrying a weight far heavier than his tailored suits.

Stress wasn't a concept for him; it was a physical, living presence, coiled around his ribs, squeezing, whispering, gnawing. Fifteen years of deadlines, boardrooms, negotiations, and self-imposed perfection had carved trenches into his body and mind. His muscles ached with tension that wouldn't relax, and his sleep was fragmented by phantom phone calls and emails he hadn't yet answered. Meals were skipped or inhaled in the office, a grim ritual that left his stomach twisted and empty. And the doctor, who had looked at him with an almost fearful kind of frankness, had laid it bare: "Keep going like this, and you won't see fifty."

Six months ago, Abraham had sat in that stark, fluorescent-lit office, the words echoing like a death sentence. He'd nodded politely, smiled, even made a joke to mask the terror curling in his gut, but inside, panic had surged like a tidal wave. Every ambition, every accolade, every meticulously built corner office and shiny BMW now felt like chains dragging him closer to the edge.

Abraham had changed nothing. Because changing would have meant admitting the truth: he had built his life on a foundation of sand. And Abraham did not admit defeat. He didn't stumble. He didn't panic. He controlled outcomes. That was his power. That was why clients came to him with cases so tangled, so toxic, that other firms wouldn't even return their calls. Bankruptcy threats that would ruin empires, corporate betrayals that smelled like suicide, he walked into the room, and suddenly, the impossible was just another Tuesday.

He could read a room like a script. He knew who was bluffing, who was scared, who thought they were clever. He spotted leverage points the moment he walked in, and he used them with surgical precision. A smirk here, a pause there, a carefully chosen word that made the other side feel exposed, vulnerable, as though the floor beneath them was giving way. No one could bluff him because he had already anticipated the bluff before it even left their lips.

In negotiations, Abraham didn't argue; he dictated. The word *no* didn't exist. There was only the position he wanted them in, and eventually, the other side had no choice but to step into it. He could make a room full of people believe that surrendering wasn't a loss, it was inevitable, elegant, even theirs. His confidence was magnetic. His reasoning was relentless. He was calm when others panicked, precise when others fumbled, sharp when others stumbled. He could tear apart a contract line by line, anticipate every counter, and still leave the other side wondering if they had ever had a chance.

It was a beautiful, terrifying kind of control. He made people feel small without raising his voice. He won with style, with intellect, with instinct honed over years of bending chaos to his will. This brilliance had made him untouchable. It had made him rich beyond reckoning. It had also, quietly, without fanfare, started to kill him.

It was 4:30 AM, and Abraham was awake because he had been awake at 4:30 every morning for the past three years. Sleep had abandoned him, quietly, one night at a time, until it became a stranger he could no longer recognize. His heart was already pounding, as if it knew the day was waiting and demanded he be ready.

For fifteen minutes, he would lie in bed, willing himself to relax, to breathe, to surrender to a morning that felt impossible to keep up with. Fifteen minutes of trying to convince his body to obey, while his mind silently cataloged every flaw, every oversight, every potential misstep. Then he gave up. Always. There was no surrender, no compromise. He rose, dressed in the quiet armor of his home office, and began the day that had already started in his head hours ago.

His therapist, the one his doctor had practically mandated after the diagnosis, called it anxiety. Abraham called it discipline.

Not stress. Not panic. Not weakness. Discipline. The kind that demanded perfection before sunrise, that turned hours of silence and darkness into advantage, that let him bend the impossible to his will while the rest of the city slept.

Even at this hour, there were fires to put out. A client in Park Forest needed a contract reviewed before a seven AM meeting. A junior associate had questions about a brief due next week. Abraham's fingers moved over the keyboard with the precision of a surgeon, cracking out responses, untangling problems, and bending every situation to his control. Emails disappeared from his inbox as quickly as they arrived; crises were neutralized before they had a chance to grow. This was his domain. This was where he was God.

Not the God his mother had worshiped in that tiny southside church, where she had held him as a baby, naming him after a man who had supposedly been faithful. Not the God who promised heaven while letting the faithful suffer on earth. Abraham hated that God. Hated the way the world seemed rigged with unfair rules, with suffering as inevitable as breath. He hated the notion of blind faith. He hated helplessness.

Without warning, his chest seized. Abraham froze mid-sentence; hands suspended over the keyboard as if caught in a trap. The tightness hit him like a fist driving into his sternum, sharp and unrelenting, cutting off his breath before he could even realize it. His lungs clawed for air; shallow, ragged, insufficient.

For a moment, panic flickered, a primal, wordless fear, but he forced himself to stay still, to breathe, to ride it out. Thirty seconds, maybe a minute, though time stretched like molasses. His vision dimmed at the edges. Beads of sweat prickled along his temples. Every instinct screamed that this was it, the cardiac event his doctor had warned him about, but it passed, as it always did, leaving only the dull ache of his own fragility.

Abraham exhaled sharply, shoulders stiff, heart still hammering, then returned to typing. The emails waited. The crises waited. The world did not pause for him, and neither would he.

By six AM, he had cleared his inbox. By six-thirty, showered, dressed, briefcase in hand, Abraham moved through his apartment like a machine, every motion precise, every decision pre-calculated. By seven, he was in his car, slicing through the early morning traffic, already three moves ahead in his head, already running the day like a script he had memorized.

The deposition at nine loomed like a battlefield. By the time he entered the conference room, Abraham had mentally mapped every angle, every possible weakness, every subtle hesitation he could exploit. But the witness was not what he expected. She sat perfectly still, posture straight, hands folded, eyes unwavering. She radiated calm, centeredness, and the quiet authority of someone who knew she was right. Abraham knew it too. She had been wronged. She had been treated unjustly. Morally, she was untouchable.

He didn't care. Morality had no place in his world. He didn't deal in right or wrong; he dealt in outcomes. His client wanted the case buried quietly, with minimal financial fallout. That was his job. Bend the reality of the situation. Make the result inevitable. That was all that mattered.

He unleashed everything in his arsenal: meticulous strategies designed to create doubt, invisible pressure meant to destabilize, angles calibrated to exploit the tiniest hint of hesitation. Every lever he pulled, every calculated move he made, bounced harmlessly off her. She was steady. Unshakable. Honest. Immovable.

By eleven-fifteen, the deposition ended. Abraham's body betrayed him in subtle ways: the headache blooming behind his eyes, the familiar tightness in his chest. He canceled his next engagement, retreated to his office, drawing the blinds, plunging the room into shadow. He sank into the leather chair, breathing shallow, trying to restore order to the chaos inside his own mind.

His phone buzzed. A text from his mother. He ignored it. She sent messages every week, always about church, family, or some gentle reminder of when he was going to visit. He loved her. He really did. But love didn't make him pick up the phone. There wasn't time. There wasn't enough space. Nostalgia and obligation were luxuries he had traded for efficiency and control years ago.

The phone buzzed again. David, this time. Abraham ignored it too, letting it sit. Then it rang. His mother. The third call this week. Abraham stared at the screen, watching it pulse with insistence. She would call back later if he didn't answer. She always did. Persistent, relentlessly, exhausting, impossibly so. That had been her way all his life. Persistent in prayer, in belief, in the certainty that her sons would turn out alright despite the world pressing down on them, despite the odds stacked against them in that Southside neighborhood.

He loved that persistence too, even if it drove him mad. But it was tinged with something else, a kind of naïve, infuriating faith in a God he could never respect. God had never been fair. Never had been just. And yet, his mother clung to Him as if the world could be fixed with prayer. She wasn't cruel, she was just…blind, innocent, stubborn in ways he had outgrown, ways he had traded for sharp edges and hard truths.

Abraham pressed the answer button on the fifth ring.

"Mom."

"Sweety, I've been trying to reach you," she said, soft and gentle, her voice carrying that quiet warmth he had always known, the one that could soothe even the sharpest edges of his mind.

"I know. Sorry. Work's been…busy."

"Busy is always your excuse," she said, lightly teasing, but there was no bite, only the warmth of a mother who knew him too well and loved him too much to let it slide.

"It's true," he said, flat, not meeting her cheer.

He heard murmurs in the background, probably the church again. She was always there, always busy with something she cared about.

"Abraham, we need to talk about David," she said, her voice steady, soft, carefully measured, as though she were wrapping her concern in a blanket so it wouldn't sting.

His brother. Two years younger. The one who followed all the rules their mother had taught them. College on a partial scholarship, honors graduate, good teaching job. Living on the Southside, still at the church, still believing in the God Abraham had long since stopped trusting. David, whom he hadn't spoken to in months despite living in the same city.

"What about David?" he asked.

"He's struggling, baby," she said, her voice lilting, gentle, patient. "He lost his job. Budget cuts, fifteen teachers let go, and he was one of them. He's looking, but…" She paused, almost tenderly, "You know how it is. And Ruth's pregnant with their third. Their savings are tight. I'm helping as much as I can, but my pension barely covers my rent…"

Abraham's mind drifted. He had heard it before: David needed help. David needed Abraham. And Abraham, rich, untouchable, in control, was expected to fix it.

"How much?" he said finally, his voice neutral.

"Abraham, it's not money," she said. "He wouldn't take it from me, and he wouldn't take it from you. What he needs…is you. Just to talk. To know you're there. That his brother is still…his brother."

It wasn't about money. It was present. Time. Emotional availability. The things Abraham had cut from his life in pursuit of control.

"I'm in the middle of something," he said, evasive. "Can we talk later?"

"When, baby? When is later?" Her voice didn't scold. It carried patience and a quiet sadness, a gentle insistence. "You've been saying that for three years. You promised Sunday dinners. You promised to meet your nieces. You promised, and…" Her tone broke slightly, warm and mournful, "you haven't. You're always in the middle of something."

Her voice wasn't angry. Not frustrated. Not demanding. Sweet. Loving. Soft, the kind of voice that could wrap you in comfort even while reminding you of your failures. Abraham felt something shift inside him, a crack in the wall he had built around himself. Not breaking. Just cracking.

"I'll call him," he said finally.

"Okay, just…be his brother. That's all anyone needs. Just show up."

They lingered on the line a few more minutes, she filling the spaces with church gossip, family updates, and invitations he had no intention of accepting. He made the right noises at the right times, years of practice showing in every tone.

When he hung up, Abraham sat in the dark of his office, feeling the weight of that small fissure, the warmth of her voice lingering, tugging at something he rarely allowed himself to feel.

He should call David. He knew he should. But what could he even offer? Money? Advice? Job leads? His carefully honed wisdom about a world that chewed people up and spat them out? None of it mattered. David didn't want that. He wanted a brother, someone who would sit with him in the struggle, not fix it with billable hours and connections. Abraham didn't know how to be that person anymore. Maybe he never had.

The afternoon passed in a blur, meetings, calls, endless grinding work to maintain his position, his reputation, his perfectly constructed life. By seven PM, most of the office had emptied. By eight, Abraham was alone on his floor, the cleaning crew moving quietly through the halls, carts squeaking, vacuums humming.

He should go home. The brief could wait until morning. He should eat something. Breakfast had been a bitter cup of coffee. Lunch hadn't happened. He should take care of himself. That's what the doctor said. That's what the therapist said. Self-care, as if his body were a car and a tune-up could fix what was breaking.

Abraham stayed at his desk. Scrolling through case files, trying not to think about David, about his mother, about the tightness curling in his chest, a chest ache that lingered longer than usual. He reached for the antacids when the phone rang. Unknown number.

He hesitated. Then picked up.

"Is this Abraham Ducksworth?"

"Yes. Who is this?"

"Mr. Ducksworth, this is Dr. Chan from Cook County Hospital. Your brother David listed you as his emergency contact. He's been admitted."

The world tilted.

"What happened?"

"He collapsed at home. His wife called an ambulance. We're running a test now, but it appears to be a significant cardiac event." The words hit him like a punch to the gut. Abraham's hands curled into fists at his sides.

"Mr. Ducksworth, you should come to the hospital… your brother is asking for you." Abraham's world tilted. His usual control, the armor of discipline and logic, felt thin, fragile.

Abraham heard himself saying he was on his way. He heard himself asking which floor, which room. Then he was standing, coat in hand, moving toward the elevator on legs that felt disconnected from his body. His brother was in the hospital. His brother had a heart attack.

David, two years younger, careful, steady, responsible, was lying in a hospital bed, hooked up to machines because his heart had failed. Just like Abraham's own body had been warning him for years.

The drive to the hospital took twenty minutes, but felt like twenty hours. Abraham's mind refused to stop. Scenarios, probabilities, outcomes, every piece of medical data he could recall, every statistic he had ever learned, every contingency plan ran in a relentless loop. Survival rates for cardiac events in men under forty. Long-term outcomes. How would the family cope if David didn't make it?

He thought of everything, except the one thing that truly mattered: David might die. And Abraham had been too busy, too consumed, too enthralled with his own success to call. Too consumed with being untouchable, precise, invincible. Too consumed to be a brother.

The hospital was a whirlwind of chaos, even at eight-thirty at night. The emergency room throbbed with people in pain; fear etched into their faces. Abraham pushed through the crowd, every step fueled by urgency, heart hammering, mind racing faster than his legs could carry him.

He reached the information desk, voice sharp, insistent. "I need to know where David Ducksworth is. Now."

The receptionist barely looked up, her tone tired but polite, a practiced patience in every word. "Cardiac unit, fourth floor. Take the elevator or stairs."

The stairwell was a blur. His pulse thundered in his ears. Each step felt like dragging his body through molasses, but he barely noticed. All that mattered was reaching his brother.

Bursting through the doors of the cardiac unit, a nurse stepped in front of him, arms folded, calm but firm. "Sir, can I help you?"

"My brother. David Ducksworth. Room three fifty-seven. He's my brother. Abraham Ducksworth," he said, words spilling over each other.

The nurse softened, reading the panic in his eyes. Her tone was gentle, measured, meant to ground him. "Mr. Ducksworth…he's stable. The next twenty-four hours are critical, but he's stable. He's asking for you. Room three fifty-seven."

Abraham nodded, barely registering her words, and moved down the hallway on autopilot. Every step felt like wading through water, every breath a labor. The fluorescent lights were harsh, too bright. The antiseptic stung his nose; it was too strong. Every sound, every movement pressed down on him.

He reached Room 357. Stopped. Stared at the door. Time slowed. He could feel the panic coiling inside him, threatening to unravel all the control he had clung to for decades.

He took a steadying breath. Tried to prepare. Tried to imagine what to say, how to be. Which version of himself belonged here, in the hospital hallway, in front of his brother, where none of his skills, his intellect, or his discipline could fix what mattered.

But there was no time to prepare. The door opened, and a woman emerged, Ruth. Her hair was loose, strands sticking to her tear-streaked cheeks. Her eyes were red, swollen from crying, and her hands instinctively cradled her swollen belly. She saw Abraham and, as if all her fear and exhaustion poured out in that instant, she stumbled toward him.

"Thank God you're here," she whispered, voice breaking, trembling.

Before he could speak, she collapsed into his arms, shuddering with silent sobs. Abraham's arms went around her instinctively, holding her, feeling the weight of her panic, the heat of her tears seeping through his suit.

"I… I'm here," he said, voice low, unsure, shaky even though he usually controlled everything. He didn't know what to do, didn't know what to say, but he held her anyway, letting her grief spill onto him, feeling it like an electric shock he couldn't turn off.

He held her in that hospital hallway and let her cry, and found that he was crying too. Not the controlled, quiet tears of someone performing grief. But the ugly, gasping, ragged sobs of someone whose carefully constructed world had just collapsed, and there was nothing left to do but hold on.

When she finally pulled back, wiping her eyes with the heel of her hand, she looked at him with something that might have been gratitude, or might have been forgiveness, or both.

"He wants to see you," she said softly. "He's been asking for you since he woke up. Go on in. I'll be right here."

Abraham nodded, not trusting himself to speak, and pushed open the door to room three fifty-seven.

The man on the bed didn't look like his brother. David had always been bigger than Abraham, not taller, but broader, stronger. The athlete to Abraham's scholar. But here, hooked up to monitors and IV lines, he looked diminished. Mortal. Vulnerable. Every line of his face, every rise and fall of his chest, reminded Abraham of childhood summers playing basketball in the alley, of snowball fights on the Southside, of late-night whispers in the room they had shared. Memories hit him like a wave: David laughing at his terrible jokes, David sharing the last slice of pie, David arguing over homework assignments, fighting off scraped knees, cheering him on when he won a spelling bee.

David's eyes opened as Abraham approached, catching the fleeting, fragile smile he had always known. For a long moment, neither spoke. They just looked at each other, two brothers who had grown up in the same house, shared the same room, survived the same neighborhood, and then diverged onto different paths. In that sterile hospital room, nostalgia hit Abraham hard, pulling him back to a simpler time when being a brother didn't require strategy, success, or armor. They had become strangers in adulthood, but here, in this quiet, fragile moment, the distance between them felt small, almost bridgeable.

"You came," David said finally, his voice a rasp, barely above a whisper. He coughed once, a small, ragged sound that made Abraham flinch.

"Of course I came. You're my brother," Abraham said, his voice low, controlled, though his chest felt tight.

"I… I wasn't sure," David said, coughing again, clutching the sheets. "Mom… she called you."

"I know. I'm sorry," Abraham said, sitting down on the edge of the bed, careful not to crowd him.

"I was going to call you. I was going to…" Abraham trailed off. He saw a small tremor running through David's thin fingers. He looked fragile, diminished, hooked up to IV lines and monitors, chest rising and falling unevenly with each weak breath. Abraham's heart clenched.

Abraham wanted to say something, anything to fix it. But what could he offer? All his skill, his knowledge, his control, useless here. David was too small, too human, too real.

"You look terrible," David rasped, voice cracking.

"Thanks," Abraham said, forcing a weak smile, even as he felt it fail. "You look… good yourself."

David let out a short laugh, coughing again, then his gaze fixed on Abraham. "I saw it," he whispered, fragile but steady. "When my heart… stopped. I saw everything. Every choice I made… every time I chose me over God, me over my family… over what actually mattered."

Abraham's hands clenched into fists at his sides. He didn't know what to say. Couldn't intervene. Couldn't fix the reality of this frail, beaten-down man he had always called his brother.

"I thought I was different from you," David continued, voice trembling. "I thought… staying on the Southside, going to church, doing what I was supposed to… it made me righteous. But I was just as prideful. Just in a different way. I thought I was in control. And then my heart stopped, and I realized… I controlled nothing. Absolutely nothing."

David closed his eyes, leaning back against the pillow, lips parted as he drew shallow, shaky breaths. Abraham watched him, heart hammering, wanting to protect him, to take the pain into himself, to trade places if he could. But he couldn't.

"Mom called you… because I asked her to," David whispered, his voice weaker still, breaking at the edges. "Because I needed to tell you… before it's too late. Before you end up in a bed like this… or worse. Abraham… you have to stop. Lay it down. All of it. The career, the control… It's killing you. Not slowly. Quickly."

Abraham opened his mouth, but the words wouldn't come. He wanted to argue. To defend his life. To convince himself, it was different for him. But he knew. He felt the tightness in his chest, the warning from years ago that he had ignored.

"I don't know how," Abraham admitted finally, voice raw, broken. "I don't know how to… let go. To surrender. Everything I am… everything I've built… It's all based on never surrendering. If I stop, I don't know what's left. I don't know who I am without it."

David's eyelids fluttered open. His hand, pale and trembling, reached for Abraham's. Abraham took it, feeling the weakness, the fragility, the life barely clinging to him.

"That's the point, man," David said, voice whisper-thin. "You're not supposed to know. You can't see the other side. That's what makes it a surrender instead of a strategy. You lay it all down… without proof, without guarantee. You trust. You let go. That's faith.

The real kind. Not Sunday school stuff. The kind that costs everything."

A single tear slid down Abraham's cheek as he gripped his brother's hand, feeling the weight of thirty-five years of control, ambition, and pride pressing down on him. Thirty-five years of running from surrender, from the test his namesake had faced. Abraham, biblical Abraham, had obeyed, had surrendered, had trusted even when the knife was raised.

Abraham Ducksworth, in this hospital room, watching his brother's chest rise and fall with each fragile breath, understood at last. Surrender wasn't a strategy. It was life or death. And for him, it was both.

David had fallen asleep—or maybe lost consciousness. Abraham wasn't sure. The monitors continued their steady beeping, a constant reminder of fragility and life balanced on a knife's edge. Nurses moved quietly around the room, checking IV lines, adjusting medication, making notes on charts, their footsteps light, their voices low and calm, almost ritualistic in contrast to Abraham's racing mind.

Ruth entered, quiet but purposeful. Her hair was pulled back in a loose braid, damp strands clinging to her face, a single streak of mascara running down her cheek. Her hands rested on her swollen belly as she knelt beside David's bed, taking his other hand in hers. She bowed her head, lips moving in whispered prayer, her voice soft but unwavering, carrying a rhythm of faith that Abraham hadn't heard in decades. Each word trembled with emotion, but she spoke with certainty, as if her pleading hands could anchor their lives.

Abraham watched her and felt a twinge he hadn't felt in years. Envy. Not for her life, not for her circumstances, but for her faith. Her ability to surrender completely, to trust that someone was listening, that someone cared, that letting go wasn't falling into nothing, but falling into hands stronger than his own.

Hours passed. Abraham stayed, rooted to the floor, refusing to leave even when nurses suggested he go home, rest, and try to sleep. He couldn't. He had to witness this, had to be present. Something deeper than David's medical crisis was breaking open inside him, something sealed for decades.

Around midnight, David's eyes flickered open. They were clearer now, more focused, though still tired, still fragile. He coughed once, a small rasp that made Abraham wince. Then he smiled, a real, small, tentative smile.

"I'm going to make it," he said, voice weak, breath uneven. "I… I don't know how I know, but this… this isn't the end. It's the beginning."

Ruth let out a cry of relief, tears spilling down her cheeks. She pressed her lips to David's hand, his forehead, his cheek, whispering thanks to God in a voice full of raw, unrestrained faith. She didn't care who heard; it was just her, and him, and the certainty that he was still here.

David turned to Abraham, his fingers trembling slightly in Abraham's grip. "You're going to make it too," he said, voice raw, fragile, yet urgent. "But only if you do what I did. Only if you let it all go, right now. Tonight. Don't wait. Don't plan. Don't manage it. That's your will trying to control surrender. You have to do it cold. Say it out loud. So, you hear it. So, God hears it."

Abraham opened his mouth, but no protest came. No excuses, no justifications about cases, clients, responsibilities. Instead, a single, trembling breath escaped, followed by words that broke him open.

"I surrender," he whispered.

The words came again, louder this time, trembling through his chest, raw and jagged. "I surrender. I give up. I can't do this anymore. I can't carry this weight. I can't control this life. I can't be my own god. I'm done. I'm done trying. I'm done managing. I'm done believing my will matters more than yours. God, if you're there… if there's mercy left for someone who's spent his whole life running… I surrender. Everything. My career, my success, my control, my life, everything. I'm laying it down. Right here. Right now. I surrender."

He sobbed violently, his whole body shaking with grief and relief, a sob that seemed to come from somewhere deeper than his chest. Ruth cried too, a mixture of relief and joy spilling from her. David, weak and exhausted, tears streaming down his face, offered a small, pained smile.

The three of them sat there, in the middle of the night, in a hospital room in Chicago, the city lights glowing faintly through the windows. They were raw, vulnerable, human. And in that vulnerability, something shifted.

The air felt different. Lighter. The weight Abraham had carried for thirty-five years, the ambition, the control, the relentless striving, lifted. Not slowly. Not gradually. But completely. And in its place was something he had never known: freedom. Terrifying, yes, but right. Real. And at the center of it, a quiet, deep, undeniable peace. Not the shallow calm that comes from having everything under control, but the profound, gut-level peace that comes from surrendering everything.

Abraham closed his eyes, still holding his brother's hand, still feeling Ruth's warmth at his side, and for the first time in decades, breathed without the weight pressing down on him.

Abraham stayed at the hospital until dawn. David slept, his breathing slow and even, the monitors beside him humming like the steady pulse of life itself. Ruth dozed in the chair by the window, one hand resting protectively on her swollen belly, the other loosely holding David's hand. Her head was tipped forward, her braid spilling over her shoulder, her eyelashes wet with tears she hadn't wiped away. Abraham watched her and felt something stir that he hadn't felt in years, envy, yes, but also longing. The kind of longing that comes from seeing someone fully trust, fully surrender, and believing that the world is listening when they pray. He wanted that. He needed that. But he didn't know how to reach it.

The room brightened slowly, gray light stretching across the linoleum floors, the sterile walls, the monitors and IV lines that had become almost holy in their constancy. Abraham's old self—the man who had spent thirty-five years bending every circumstance to his will, the man who had believed control was salvation, was gone. Dead in room three fifty-seven sometime around midnight. The new Abraham, raw and unarmed, was fragile, trembling, but alive. He didn't know what surrender would demand of him. He didn't know if God would ask him to walk away from the firm, to give away his wealth, to live like David on the Southside, or if He would ask nothing at all. For the first time in his life, Abraham realized he didn't need to know.

He only needed to be present. He only needed to listen.

The sun rose higher, brushing the skyline with light. Abraham stretched, feeling every stiff muscle, and glanced down at his brother. David's face was calm now, peaceful even, and Abraham's chest swelled with gratitude. Not for the hospital, not for the doctors, not for the machines keeping his brother alive—but for David himself. For his courage. For the way David had risked being rejected to tell Abraham the truth, the way he had forced him to see what he refused to admit: that all of Abraham's life, all of his striving, his control, his brilliance, had been empty without surrender.

He walked to the window and looked down on Chicago. The streets were filling with cars, the sidewalks with people rushing to appointments, meetings, obligations. He had been one of them yesterday, absorbed in the motion, convinced that his will could bend the world. Now it looked different. It was noise, distraction, the desperate clamor of humanity trying to assert control over a universe that obeyed its own rules. He could almost hear the trumpet Michael Flowers had heard in his apartment, the warning of the end, the signal that time was slipping. He didn't hear it yet, but he felt it coming. And for the first time, he didn't need to fear it.

His phone buzzed. A text from his assistant reminded him of the nine o'clock partners' meeting. Abraham stared at it, then slid it into his pocket without a thought. The meeting would happen without him. The cases would go on without him. The world would spin without him. And he would remain here, in the quiet of the hospital room, with his brother, with Ruth, with God finally pulling at the corners of his attention.

Surrender wasn't a single act. It wasn't a one-time decision. It was daily, terrifying, and complete. It was laying down the life he had built, every success, every achievement, every shred of control, and trusting that it didn't all have to be on his shoulders. Abraham Ducksworth spent thirty-five years thinking his name was a burden. Now he understood it. His namesake had been willing to sacrifice his son. Abraham had to be willing to sacrifice himself—his ambition, his control, his carefully constructed world. And in that complete surrender, he would find freedom. He would find peace. He would find God. And when the trumpet sounded, he would be ready.

How close do you have to get to the edge before you finally lay it down? Or will you wait until it's too late? Until the trumpet sounds and you're still clutching your will with white-knuckle determination, still believing you know better than God, still convinced you can manage your own salvation.

There is no managing this. There is no control in this. There is only surrender. Complete, total surrender. The kind that costs you everything and gives you back something you can't even name until you've experienced it.

Abraham found it in a hospital room at midnight. He felt it in the quiet beeping of the monitors, in the soft weight of his brother's hand in his, in the small, steady rhythm of Ruth's breathing as she dozed in the chair by the window. The surrender was not metaphorical, not symbolic. It was raw, real, unavoidable. It was the complete letting go of a life built on control, on ambition, on the stubborn belief that he could bend the world to his will. And in that letting go, he discovered something he hadn't known he was capable of feeling: freedom.

Where will you find it? When will you stop running? How much time do you think you have left? Abraham didn't know. He didn't need to know. All he knew was that he had finally, terrifyingly, beautifully let go.

CHAPTER 3:
RESTORING OUR SANITY

"You will keep him in perfect peace, whose mind is stayed on You, because he trusts in You."
- Isaiah 26:3

Isaac Ellis was arguing with a toaster. Not in the abstract sense. Not as a metaphor for a failing life or a morning gone wrong. He was arguing with an actual toaster, chrome, two-sliced, mildly reflective, standing in the narrow galley kitchen of his apartment at exactly seven forty-three on a Tuesday morning.

"You had one job," Isaac said, voice sharp, finger pointed like an accusation that might finally stick. "One. Job."

The toaster answered the way it always did: by doing absolutely nothing.

The smell of burnt bread lingered in the air, bitter and accusing. Inside the toaster, two bagel halves sat imprisoned, their tops scorched to a uniform black while the bottoms remained pale, soft, and offensively underdone. It was an imbalance that felt personal.

"Toast bread," Isaac continued, lowering his voice as if reason might succeed where volume had failed. "That's it. That's your entire purpose. You don't cook. You don't create. You don't multitask.

You toast." He reached down and jabbed the lever. It refused to budge. Of course it did.

Isaac exhaled slowly and straightened, rubbing at his temple. The kitchen was quiet except for the hum of the refrigerator and the faint ticking of the wall clock, both of which felt like they were watching him. Judging. Waiting.

"I maintain you," he said, softer now. "I clean your crumb tray. I don't overload your outlet. I never once asked you to do more than you're capable of."

The toaster reflected his face at him, tired eyes, unshaven jaw, the look of a man who had woken up already behind schedule and was now negotiating with kitchenware.

Silence.

Isaac was not suffering from a psychotic break. He did not believe kitchen appliances could talk back, argue their case, or offer apologies. He knew the toaster was just a machine, incapable of intent or malice. That knowledge, however, did nothing to stop him from continuing the argument, from gesturing emphatically at the faintly smoking remains of what had been a perfectly good bagel, or from feeling a very real, very sharp anger at this small chrome object that had betrayed him. Because it wasn't really about the bagel, it was never about the bagel.

Isaac Ellis was forty-two years old. He had been divorced for six years, long enough for the shock to have worn off but not long enough for the quiet to feel normal. He was the father of two teenagers who lived with their mother in the suburbs and texted him maybe once a week if he was lucky, usually when they needed something or were answering a question he had already asked twice. He read their messages carefully, as if there might be something hidden between the lines, some sign that they missed him the way he missed them, and then he put his phone face down and tried not to think about it too much.

He worked as a middle manager at an insurance company, which meant his job consisted mostly of translating bad news downward and blaming upward. He had just enough authority to be held responsible when something went wrong and not nearly enough power to prevent it from going wrong in the first place. His days were filled with emails that required careful wording, meetings that ended without decisions, and problems he was expected to solve using tools he wasn't given.

He lived alone in a one-bedroom apartment in the northern suburbs of Evanston, a place that smelled faintly of mildew no matter how many air fresheners he bought or windows he opened. The carpet was worn thin in the places where he walked most, and the walls carried the muted sounds of other people's lives, including televisions, footsteps, and laughter that reminded him he was alone, without ever directly saying so. He drove a twelve-year-old Honda that made concerning noises when he turned too sharply or accelerated too fast, sounds he pretended not to hear because he couldn't afford to find out what they meant.

Mostly, Isaac was tired. Not the kind of tired that came from a late night or a hard week, but a deeper, heavier exhaustion that settled into him and stayed there. The kind that made mornings feel like obligations and evenings feel like failures. He couldn't remember the last time he had woken up feeling rested, or the last time he had gone to sleep without a low-level sense of dread about the next day waiting for him.

His life had become a collection of small frustrations, none of them catastrophic on their own, but relentless in their accumulation. Bills that weren't overdue yet but hovered constantly at the edge of his thoughts. Work emails multiplied faster than he could answer them. A freezer full of microwave dinners bought on sale and forgotten about. Clothes that needed washing, dishes that needed cleaning, phone calls that needed returning, and appointments that needed scheduling. It was a life that functioned on paper and felt completely out of control in practice.

And that morning, all of it, the exhaustion, the disappointment, the quiet sense of failure, had condensed itself into one burned bagel and the toaster that had burned it.

Isaac grabbed the toaster, unplugging it with more force than necessary, and shoved it into the cabinet beneath the sink, where he kept cleaning supplies and things he didn't want to look at but couldn't quite bring himself to throw away. He shut the door hard and stood there for a moment, staring at the counter, the smell of burnt bread still lingering in the air. Out of sight, out of mind. It wasn't a solution, but it was the closest thing he had.

That had become his primary coping mechanism: if you didn't look at it, it didn't exist. At least, that was the rule he lived by. Push things into drawers. Shut cabinet doors. Leave emails unanswered just long enough to convince himself they weren't urgent yet. It worked, in the way denial often does, briefly, imperfectly, and at a cost. Because the truth was, it all still existed. Every unpaid bill, every unfinished task, every unspoken fear. The chaos didn't disappear just because he refused to meet its gaze; it simply waited, patient and accumulating.

Isaac stood in the middle of his kitchen, staring at the stretch of empty counter where the toaster had been, and felt something give way inside him. It wasn't the dramatic kind of breaking, the kind that announced itself with collapse or tears or raised voices. It wasn't like the rupture Abraham had experienced in that hospital room, sharp and unmistakable. This was smaller, quieter, almost polite. A subtle fracture. But it carried weight. It changed something.

He realized, with a slow and unwelcome clarity, that he was losing his grip. Not in a way that would earn a diagnosis or land him in a hospital bed. Nothing so visible or easily named. He was losing it in the spaces between things, in his thoughts, in his reactions, in the way his mind latched onto trivial failures and treated them like personal catastrophes. He was losing the ability to think clearly, to respond proportionally, to tell the difference between what mattered and what merely demanded attention.

That terrified him more than the anger ever had. Because if a burned bagel could send him spiraling, if a broken toaster could feel like betrayal, then what happened when something real went wrong? What happened when the crisis wasn't small or domestic or ridiculous, but permanent and undeniable? If he couldn't distinguish between inconvenience and disaster, how was he supposed to navigate anything larger than this kitchen, this morning, this moment?

Because Isaac had heard the stories. Everyone had, by now. They had started circulating about a week ago, whispers at first, half-formed and easy to ignore. Urban legends. The kind of thing you heard third-hand, from someone who knew someone who swore it had really happened. Stories about a blackout in Chicago that lasted three days. Stories about a sound people heard, a trumpet blast that seemed to come from everywhere and nowhere at once. Stories about empty clothes left on sidewalks, about people who vanished without explanation, about a city gone silent in a way that defied natural law.

It sounded like an episode of *The Twilight Zone*. And Isaac dismissed them. Of course he did. They were obviously internet conspiracy theories, a digital-age version of campfire ghost stories. People loved drama. People loved believing they were living through something significant, something that would make their ordinary lives feel important. It was all just noise. Just another distraction in a world already drowning in them.

Except the stories didn't stop.

They kept coming. More cities. More blackouts. More reports of that sound. Different sources, different voices, all repeating the same details with unsettling consistency. And yesterday, Isaac's own power had flickered. Just for a moment. Just long enough to make his computer reboot and erase twenty minutes of work. Nothing catastrophic. Nothing worth panicking over. But enough to linger in his thoughts, quietly, like an unanswered question.

The lights had dimmed. The steady hum of electricity wavered, faltered for just a moment, and for thirty seconds, Isaac sat frozen in his cubicle, his fingers hovering over the keyboard, heart thudding in a way that felt too loud, too exposed. He wondered if this was it.

If the stories were true. If the careful compartments he had built around his life, the fragile order he maintained over bills, emails, laundry, and unpaid obligations, were about to be swept away by something far bigger, far beyond his control.

Then the lights flickered back. The hum returned. Everything seemed normal again. And Isaac, eager to cling to reason, told himself it was nothing. Just the grid being unreliable. Just another small frustration to add to the pile. The kind of thing you ignore until it disappears from memory.

But the fear didn't disappear. It stayed, heavy and unrelenting, pressing against his chest like a stone, cold and hard, making it difficult to breathe. The rational part of him tried to insist it was absurd, ridiculous even. But the part that felt, that *knew*, whispered that maybe it wasn't. Maybe the blackout wasn't random. Maybe the stories weren't just noise. Maybe something was really happening. Something big. Something he was not remotely prepared for.

He left his kitchen without eating. The smell of burnt bagel lingered faintly in the air, and he ignored it, shoved it to the corners of his mind like he always did. He grabbed his keys, his wallet, and his phone, already buzzing with work emails he didn't want to read, and stepped into the cold morning. His drive to the office was mechanical, his hands on the wheel moving through familiar streets, while his mind spun through scenarios he didn't want to consider, scenarios that felt too large, too impossible.

What if the stories were true? What if there really was some kind of apocalyptic event unfolding, quiet at first, invisible until it hit? What if the trumpet everyone whispered about, the one that sounded from nowhere and everywhere at once, was the trumpet? The one from the Book of Revelation, signaling the end of time, the coming of judgment? The thought made his stomach tighten and his throat dry. He had spent his life managing small, manageable chaos, and now the chaos might be cosmic. And he was utterly, painfully, unprepared.

Isaac wasn't religious, or, more accurately, he hadn't been in any meaningful way for twenty years. He had grown up going to church, like most kids in his generation. His parents were casual believers, the type who showed up on Christmas and Easter and maybe a handful of Sundays in between. They had sent him to Sunday school, where he learned the basic stories: Noah and the ark, David and Goliath, Jesus and the cross. At ten, it had all seemed distant and vaguely boring, like history lessons about people who lived so long ago they might as well have been fictional.

He had stopped going to church when he went to college. Not because of any crisis of faith, not because he had rejected it in some dramatic, conscious way, he had simply stopped. There were better things to do on Sunday mornings. Sleep. Study. Eventually, work. Church had faded from his life the way childhood things do, replaced by adult concerns: career advancement, mortgage payments, marriage.

When the kids were born, Denise had wanted them to find a church. She said it would be good for them, give them a foundation, a sense of community. Isaac had agreed in principle, but never actually visited a single church. There was always something more pressing, always a reason to put it off until next week, next month, next year. And then the marriage had collapsed, for reasons that still weren't entirely clear to him.

Denise had said he was never really present, even when he was physically there. That he lived in his head, lost in work and constant, low-level stress about things that didn't matter. That he sounded like Isaac, looked like Isaac, but wasn't really there. She had been right. Of course, she had been right. He hadn't known how to turn off the noise long enough to actually be present, to inhabit a shared life with another person. So, she left. Took the kids. Started a new life that, from the outside, looked remarkably similar to the old one, except Isaac wasn't in it.

That had been six years ago. Six years of living alone, working too much, accumulating chaos. Six years of promising himself he would get his life together, make changes, find some kind of peace or purpose, or at least stability. Six years of burned bagels and arguments with toasters.

The office was its usual controlled pandemonium: phones ringing, keyboards clicking, the ambient noise of dozens of people trying to look busy even when they weren't. Isaac navigated to his cubicle, logged into his computer, and stared at his email inbox. One hundred and forty-seven unread messages. He had cleared it completely three days ago. One hundred and forty-seven new fires to put out, new problems to solve, new evidence that no matter how hard he worked, he would never, ever get ahead of it all.

Isaac closed his email without reading a single message. He couldn't do it today. He just couldn't. The machinery of his life, the endless requirements, obligations, responsibilities—felt suddenly unbearable, like trying to bail water out of a sinking ship with a teaspoon. Technically possible. Practically pointless.

His phone buzzed. A text from his daughter, Ella. The first communication he'd had from her in two weeks.

"Dad, can you send money for the field trip? I need it by Friday."

No greeting. No, *how are you?* No acknowledgment that two weeks had passed since they had last spoken. Just a demand. Because that was what Isaac had become to his children. ATM. Utility. A source of occasional financial support and nothing else.

He stared at the text for a long moment, trying to summon a response that might maintain some connection, some evidence that he was more than a bank account, more than a background fixture in their lives. But his mind was too chaotic, too full of noise, too cluttered with burned bagels, unpaid bills, fears about trumpets and blackouts, and the end of the world.

After five minutes of deliberation, he typed two words:

"How much?"

Functional. Transactional. Empty.

Ella responded immediately:

"Seventy-five dollars."

Isaac closed his eyes. Seventy-five dollars. He had it. Barely. If he didn't buy groceries this week. If nothing unexpected came up. If his car didn't need repairs. If, if, if.

He typed another response:

"I'll send it tonight."

Then he set his phone face down on his desk and tried not to think about the fact that his daughter hadn't said thank you. That she wouldn't say thank you. Somewhere along the way, he realized, he had trained his children to see him as an obligation, a source of money, rather than a parent to have a relationship with.

How did it come to this? How had life become this accumulation of small failures and disappointments? How had he lost control of everything that mattered while still maintaining the fragile appearance of being functional? The question hung in the air, unanswerable, and Isaac felt a quiet, aching sadness settle in his chest, heavier than the emails, heavier than the unpaid bills, heavier than the world outside his cubicle. He wondered if it would ever lift.

Isaac stood so abruptly his chair shot backward, wheels shrieking before slamming into the cubicle wall with a dull, accusing thud.

Peter, in the next cubicle, leaned over the partition, eyebrows knitting   together.
"You okay, man?"

Isaac didn't trust his voice. If he opened his mouth, something ugly might come out: anger, panic, the truth, so he said nothing. He walked away from his desk, past the glowing monitors and half-empty coffee mugs, down the narrow hallway where the air felt thick and stale. He pushed through the break room, ignored the microwave's shrill beeping, and shoved open the back door that led to the parking lot.

Cold air hit his face like a slap.

He sucked it in greedily, as if he'd been underwater too long. His chest rose and fell too fast, breaths shallow and uneven. His hands trembled, fingers curling and uncurling like they didn't belong to him anymore. The fluorescent lights, the ringing phones, the endless pings of incoming emails, all of it still buzzed in his skull even out here, as if the building had branded itself into his nervous system.

This was insane. He was having a breakdown over a burnt bagel and a text message from his daughter. This wasn't normal.

This wasn't okay. He stood in the middle of the parking lot, asphalt stretching beneath his feet, the morning cool and gray, the kind of overcast autumn day Chicago specialized in, the sky heavy and indifferent. Traffic murmured beyond the lot. Somewhere overhead, a plane roared past, carrying people who were going somewhere, doing something, living lives that seemed impossibly intact.

The world kept moving. Isaac felt like he was coming apart at the seams.

He pressed his palms together, tried to steady himself, but all he felt was exhaustion so deep it scared him. He couldn't remember the last time he'd felt *functional*. Only busy. Only numb. Only bracing for the next thing.

And for the first time, standing there under a dull gray sky, Isaac wondered if he had already been broken long before today, and this was simply the moment his body finally refused to keep the secret.

Isaac pulled out his phone and did something he hadn't done in probably five years. His fingers felt clumsy, slightly numb, as he unlocked the screen. A thin sheen of sweat had formed along his hairline, despite the cool air, and he wiped his forehead with the sleeve of his jacket before opening the browser. He hesitated, then typed *churches near me*, each letter feeling heavier than it should have. When he hit search, his breath caught, shallow and tight.

The results filled the screen almost instantly. Dozens of churches. Catholic. Protestant. Non-denominational. Big ones, small ones, contemporary ones with stage lights and bands, traditional ones with steeples and wooden pews. A buffet of religious options for the spiritually hungry. Or, in Isaac's case, the spiritually desperate.

Another bead of sweat slid down his temple. His shoulders were tense, pulled up toward his ears as if he were bracing for something. He shifted his weight from one foot to the other, the phone slick in his hand, and tapped the first result.

North Shore Community Church.

The website loaded smoothly, with clean lines and neutral colors. Service times dare isplayed prominently, as if designed to remove every possible barrier. A smiling pastor filled the screen, dressed in a casual button-down shirt, relaxed, approachable. Beneath his photo were testimonials, people talking about how this church had changed their lives, how they had found purpose and peace.

It all looked so normal.

So friendly.

So safe.

Isaac's chest tightened. He felt it physically, like an invisible hand pressing inward. Sweat gathered at his brow again, his pulse loud in his ears. He imagined himself walking through those doors, standing out immediately, exposed. He didn't know the rules anymore. Didn't know what to wear, where to sit, when to stand, what words were expected of him. Didn't know if there was some unspoken protocol for people who had been gone for twenty years and suddenly showed up because their life had collapsed in a parking lot before noon.

He locked the screen and lowered the phone. His hand shook slightly as he did. What was he even looking for? Forgiveness for things he couldn't undo? Community, when he barely trusted himself to speak? Answers to questions he wasn't sure he wanted voiced out loud? Or some miraculous solution that would sweep in and organize the chaos of his life into something clean and manageable?

Churches didn't fix chaos. At least, that was what Isaac had always believed. They gave people a place to dress it up, to tuck the mess out of sight for an hour and pretend it wasn't there. He had grown up watching it happen, men and women who arrived on Sunday mornings looking calm and gentle, voices soft, smiles practiced, only to return to their ordinary lives unchanged. The same anger. The same pettiness. The same quiet confusion. Faith had seemed less like transformation and more like routine, another role people learned to play.

For most of his life, Isaac had been certain he wanted no part of it. Church felt like an obligation masquerading as meaning, order layered over chaos without ever touching its source. He had told himself he was better off without it, that clarity came from discipline and self-control, from handling things on his own.

But standing alone in the parking lot, that certainty began to loosen.

The thought came softly, almost against his will. Maybe he had missed something. Maybe in his exhaustion and stubborn determination to carry everything himself, he had dismissed something that mattered. He had spent years acting as his own authority, trusting only his judgment, believing that if he worked harder and thought clearly enough, he could keep his life aligned. Yet here he was, breath uneven, hands damp, feeling as though the ground beneath him had quietly shifted.

The chaos he'd been managing so carefully no longer felt accidental.

He remained where he was, the city humming around him, as a deeper fear surfaced, one that had been sitting just below his awareness since the power flickered the day before. It wasn't sharp or sudden. It was heavy. A sense that something was coming, something larger than his daily failures, and that he was not ready for it. The feeling spread through him now, no longer content to stay buried.

What unsettled him most was the possibility that the disorder in his life ran deeper than missed deadlines or fatigue. That it wasn't something he could fix by reorganizing his days or tightening his grip. The idea left him feeling strangely exposed, as if the noise inside him had grown so constant that it drowned out everything else.

And if that were true, if his inner world had become this cluttered, this disoriented, how would he recognize God's voice if it ever reached him? How would he know the difference between something that mattered and another demand pulling at his attention?

The question lingered, unanswered.

A memory rose from childhood, fragile and half-formed, a Sunday school story he barely remembered except for its meaning: a man driven mad by demons, living among tombs, lost to himself, until Jesus restored him, and the Scripture said he was found afterward sitting at His feet, clothed and in his right mind. The words lodged in Isaac's chest and broke something open.

That was what he needed, not a better routine, not another solution, not even repaired relationships, but his mind back, his inner world quiet enough to breathe again. He had tried to fix himself for years, for decades, believing discipline and effort would be enough, and the proof of that failure was this moment, his hands shaking, his vision blurring, his body giving out as he sank to his knees on the cold asphalt of the parking lot.

The impact barely registered. His shoulders folded inward, his breath tearing out of him in uneven gasps as tears spilled freely, uncontained, his palms pressed to the ground as if to keep himself from disappearing altogether. He lifted his face toward the gray, indifferent sky, not knowing how to pray, not knowing the words or the rules, only knowing that he was desperate, undone, emptied of every illusion of control, and the only truth he could form fell from his mouth in a broken whisper: he couldn't do this anymore, he didn't know what was happening to him, but he could not keep living like this.

Isaac stayed on his knees, the words spilling out of him in a rush he couldn't slow, his mind a tangled, aching mess he no longer had the strength to organize, everything broken and overlapping and too loud to hold, his voice hitching as he admitted he didn't even know who he was talking to, whether the words were landing anywhere or dissolving into the open sky, but if there was a God at all, if there was any mercy left for someone who had made such a quiet disaster of his life, then he needed help, not later, not eventually, but now, because he needed his mind back, needed the chaos to stop long enough for him to breathe, and when he said please it came out as a sob he couldn't contain, his throat tightening until the word barely made it past his lips, his shoulders shaking as tears fell freely, blurring the asphalt beneath him while his hands pressed uselessly against his thighs as if grounding himself might keep him from coming apart completely.

He stayed there like that for a long moment, chest heaving, humiliated and exposed, painfully aware of how small he must look if anyone were watching, and when the intensity finally ebbed he wiped at his face with the sleeve of his expensive dress shirt, the fabric streaked and damp, drawing in a deep, unsteady breath as he tried to gather himself, half-expecting something dramatic to happen, a voice, a sign, a sudden wave of peace, but nothing came, no heavens opening, no instant healing, no clean resolution to the mess he'd confessed, and yet as he remained there on the cold ground, something subtle shifted inside him.

And in that quiet, fragile as a held breath, he felt the first trace of himself return.

To the sky, to whoever might be listening, he whispered the only thing he could manage: one thing at a time. That was a start. A foothold. Something he could actually do.

He walked back into the office, past the hum of fluorescent lights and the mountain of unread emails, and for the first time in weeks, he didn't open his inbox. He sat down, opened a blank document, and typed two words at the top:

Sanity List.

Then he began to write.

Things that make me crazy:

- Trying to control everything.
- Feeling like I'm failing my kids.
- Worrying about money I don't have.

He paused, reading it over, feeling the weight of it and the absurdity of it all. For years, he had let these things spin him into panic, wasting energy he could never get back.

Then he wrote what he could actually control.

Things I actually have control over:

- How I respond to my daughter.
- Whether I ask for help.
- Whether I admit I'm not okay.

Even writing it felt like relief. He was finally naming the truth he had been avoiding: he needed help. He couldn't do it alone. The list wasn't a miracle. It didn't erase the chaos. But it was a start, a quiet acknowledgment that admitting he was broken was not failure. It was the first step toward being whole again.

This was the beginning of sanity. Not solving all his problems. Not fixing his life overnight. But creating some kind of order in the chaos. Distinguishing between what was his to carry and what wasn't. Admitting that he had been trying to be Atlas, holding up a world that was never his responsibility to hold in the first place.

His phone buzzed again. Another text from Ella,

"Did you send it yet?"

The old Isaac, the Isaac from this morning, would have felt his blood pressure spike. He would have felt anger at the demanding tone, guilt that he hadn't sent it immediately, and anxiety over whether he actually had the money to send. But this Isaac, the one who had just spent an hour writing down what he could and couldn't control, felt something different. Clarity.

He couldn't control his daughter's tone. Couldn't control whether she appreciated him, or whether she saw him as more than just a bank account. Couldn't control their relationship by himself. That was on his list of things outside his control. But he could control his response. That was on his list of things within his control.

He opened a new message and typed carefully:

"I'll send it tonight as I said. How are you doing?"

It was a small thing. Just four words, but they carried intention. A step toward being a father, not just a function. A choice to be present, not transactional. He hesitated a moment before pressing send, then exhaled.

Ella didn't respond right away. Maybe she wouldn't respond at all. That, too, was outside his control. And yet, Isaac felt lighter.

The rest of the day passed in an unusual calm. Isaac worked through his emails one by one, focusing on what mattered and letting the rest wait. When a coworker brought a new problem, he listened, asked a few clear questions, and either dealt with it, delegated it, or let it go. For the first time in months, maybe years, he was functioning, not perfectly, not without stress, but with a quiet order inside him that had been missing for far too long.

When he got home, he made a sandwich, transferred money to Ella's account, and then did something he hadn't done in years: he cleaned. Really cleaned. Dishes washed and put away, laundry sorted and folded, trash taken out, old food tossed, the bathroom scrubbed, the bed remade with fresh sheets. Three hours later, the apartment was unrecognizable, a clear reflection of the shift that had started in the parking lot that morning. Order. Space. Sanity.

Isaac stood in the middle of his kitchen, exhausted, and saw the toaster under the sink where he had shoved it that morning. He pulled it out and laughed, not bitterly, not angrily, but genuinely, the kind of laughter that comes from finally understanding something you've been missing. He had been fighting everyone and everything because he had been fighting himself. The chaos around him was nothing more than a mirror of the chaos inside. And for the first time, he understood that the real work, real peace, wouldn't come from organizing or controlling anything. It would come from surrendering, from admitting he wasn't enough on his own.

Isaac sat up in bed, the sheets crisp and clean, the apartment around him finally reflecting the order he had created. He was in a gray cotton T-shirt, the sleeves rolled slightly above his elbows, and navy sweatpants, the kind he always reached for when he needed comfort more than style. His bare feet pressed against the cool hardwood floor, the faint smell of soap and lemon cleaner still lingering from the evening's cleaning spree.

He folded his hands in front of him, resting them lightly on his knees, and let his eyes drift shut.

"Okay… I don't even know if you're listening," he murmured, his voice rough at first. "But if you are, I need to say this. I can't… I can't do it alone. I've been trying, and look where it's gotten me."

A pause. His shoulders slumped slightly.

"I don't have to carry it all. I don't have to keep my mind spinning; I keep everything in order by myself. Not anymore."

He took a deep breath, letting it tremble out slowly.

"Thank you for today. Thank you for… showing me I don't have to live like that anymore. Thank you for letting me feel my mind… clear again, even if it's just a little."

He leaned forward slightly, resting his forehead on his folded hands, elbows on his knees. The faint hum of the city came through the window, distant, indifferent. The apartment felt safe, quiet, his breath slowing.

"And… please," he added, almost a whisper, "keep showing me what matters. Help me be ready. Help me… not miss it again. I'll be able to respond. Please don't let me go back to the chaos. Don't let me forget this. Keep my mind clear. Keep me sane. In Jesus' name."

He added that last part almost as an afterthought, a half-remembered formula from childhood prayers, but it felt right.

When he finally lifted his head, his eyes opened slowly. The room was unchanged, the world still spinning outside. But inside him, something had shifted. A little more clarity, a little more peace. And it felt… real.

Isaac couldn't control whether he fit in, or whether he would feel comfortable, or whether something dramatic would happen. But he could control whether he walked through the door. That was enough.

He got out of his car, locked it, and walked toward the entrance. A volunteer held the door for him, smiling and handing him a program. "Here you go," she said warmly.

"Thanks," Isaac muttered, taking it and nodding. He stepped inside.

The lobby was bright, bustling with people chatting in small groups, children running past, the hum of energy everywhere. Music drifted from the sanctuary. Organized chaos, but alive, purposeful. These people were here for something real, something that mattered. Isaac slipped toward the back corner, wanting to observe, not be noticed.

The service began. They sang songs he didn't know. He stood when others stood, sat when they sat, followed the motions, careful not to draw attention.

Then the pastor spoke. Young, casual in jeans and a button-down, confident but calm. Isaac felt immediately that he was speaking directly to him.

"God specializes in taking broken things and making them whole," the pastor said, his voice steady. "He restores what we've shattered through pride, through stubborn insistence on control, through trying to fix everything ourselves. The first step toward real change is admitting you can't do it alone. You've been trying, haven't you?"

Isaac's chest tightened. He felt as if someone had read his mind. Every crack, every failure he'd tried to hide, every chaotic, sleepless morning, it was all being named, gently but unmistakably.

"And I know some of you are carrying heavy chaos right now," the pastor continued. "Maybe it's in your home, your work, your relationships. Maybe it's in your own heart. But God can bring order to it. One step at a time. One surrender at a time."

Isaac felt warmth flood him. Not the heat of excitement, not adrenaline, but something deeper, slower, like cracks in a wall slowly filling with mortar. Every broken piece of his life, every humiliation, every failure he'd lived with silently, it was starting to heal, slowly, gradually, in a way he could feel.

"Listen closely," the pastor said, leaning slightly forward. "In the days ahead, we're going to need clear minds. We're going to need spiritual sanity. Chaos is coming, maybe not today, maybe not this week, but soon. And when the trumpet sounds, the only ones who will be ready will be the ones who have learned to quiet the noise and hear God's voice clearly."

Isaac's breath caught. The words weren't frightening. They weren't threatening. They were precise, undeniable. Recognition. Confirmation. Every blackout, every silence, every supernatural story he'd brushed off, every personal breakdown, it wasn't random. It was leading to something. And he might have only days, or weeks, or months to get his mind right, to restore his sanity, to clear the chaos enough to hear clearly when the moment came.

The service drew to a close with another song. Isaac's knees felt heavy. The pastor stepped to the front, eyes scanning the sanctuary, voice softening but firm.

"If anyone here wants to accept Jesus," he said, "if you want to let Him restore your brokenness, to take the chaos in your life and bring clarity, I invite you to come forward. Even if you've been gone a long time. Even if you feel like you don't deserve it. Come. Take one step. Let God meet you where you are."

Isaac had never walked to the front of a church in his life. Even as a kid, he had been too self-conscious, too aware of everyone watching, too convinced that anyone walking forward was somehow more broken, more dramatic, more in need than he was. But now, seated at the back, looking at the small line of people moving toward the altar, something inside him shifted.

Everyone is that broken, he realized. Everyone is that desperate. The only difference is whether you're willing to admit it.

His heart pounded. His leg felt like lead. His hands itched with nerves, and he could feel the sweat prickling along his spine. *I can't do this,* he thought. *I'll make a fool of myself. They'll see everything I've been trying to hide.*

But then a small voice in the back of his mind reminded him of the morning, the parking lot, the list he had written, the clean apartment, the clarity he had felt. *One thing at a time,* it whispered. *You can do this one thing.*

So he stood. His legs wobbled under him, but he forced himself to move. One step, then another. The aisle stretched ahead, polished floor reflecting the soft light, people murmuring as he passed. His throat felt tight, his chest heavy, but he kept walking, each step a tiny act of courage, each step a quiet defiance of the fear that had always held him back.

He told himself: *I can do this. I can admit I need help. I can stop pretending I'm fine. This is enough.*

By the time he reached the front, a few others had already gathered there. The pastor looked at him with a calm, steady smile, no judgment, only welcome. He stepped forward and placed a hand lightly on Isaac's shoulder.

"What brought you up here today, friend?" the pastor asked.

Isaac couldn't look up. His eyes were fixed on the carpet, tracing the worn fibers as they could somehow ground him. His chest felt tight, his throat raw, and every step he'd taken to get here made him feel exposed. He swallowed hard.

"I… I didn't mean to come up here," he said, voice low, trembling. "I almost… almost stayed in my car. I didn't think I could do it."

He paused, fingers clenching into fists at his sides.

"This morning… I burnt a bagel. And I just… lost it. I don't know why, I don't even… it was stupid." His voice cracked. "And I stood there… in the parking lot, and I… I prayed. I didn't even know what to say. I just… I told God I can't do this. I can't keep doing everything myself."

His chest heaved. He pressed his palms together in front of him, still looking at the floor, feeling the heat of shame in his face.

"And then… I went back to my desk, and I made a list. Things I can't control. Things I can control. I cleaned my apartment… really cleaned it. Dishes, trash, laundry… everything. I thought… maybe if the outside was in order, I could feel a little order inside."

He swallowed again, voice catching on the next words.

His shoulders slumped. He shook his head.

"But the truth… the real truth… is my mind is a mess."

He said it like a confession, like he'd been carrying it for decades.

"I've been trying to fix it on my own... and I... I can't. I can't do it. I can't be my own answer. I... I need help. I can't... I just can't do this anymore."

He exhaled shakily, the words leaving him exhausted, raw, trembling. He kept his eyes down, waiting for the judgment he always assumed would come.

The pastor's hand stayed on Isaac's shoulder. His voice was calm, steady, the kind of voice that made it hard to feel judged, no matter how exposed he was.

"Friend," the pastor said gently, "That's the most honest prayer I have ever heard; you don't have to hide anything here. None of us does. There's no expectation, no performance. You're safe. Right here, right now."

Isaac's eyes stayed on the floor. His chest tightened. He thought he was different. Broken in ways no one else could understand. He had imagined the others watching him, thinking him pathetic, weak, incapable. He felt fragile, like a child standing in front of a crowd.

"Let's pray together," the pastor said softly. "If you're willing."

And they did. The pastor's words rose in a steady cadence. Isaac murmured his own, messy, raw, unpolished prayers. Other people in the circle murmured theirs as well.

Nothing dramatic happened. No visions. No voices. No sudden flood of clarity. But when Isaac finally opened his eyes, everything felt... different.

The world around him looked sharper, clearer. Less chaotic. More ordered. Like someone had adjusted the focus on a camera lens, and suddenly the blur was gone.

And then he noticed the people around him, not watching him as if he were the only broken one, but *seeing themselves* in him. In his trembling hands, his shaking voice, his honesty, they recognized their own fear and exhaustion. And in that recognition, there was gratitude. Every pair of eyes said it silently: *Thank you.*

Because they hadn't dared to stand there, to let the weight of everything fall out in words. But he had. And in standing there, pouring himself out, he had allowed everyone else to see that they weren't alone.

Isaac realized then that he wasn't different. He wasn't the only one broken. He was part of something bigger: people learning to admit their brokenness, people learning to let go of the illusion of control, people daring to hope that maybe, just maybe, restoration was possible.

For the first time in years, he felt it: safe, seen, and not alone. And it was… enough.

Isaac walked toward his car, chest still full from the service, a strange mix of calm and anticipation in his limbs. The sunlight felt sharper, clearer, as if the world had shifted just slightly.

Then his phone beeped. He froze, hand hovering over the handle. He unlocked it and saw the message. Shock rooted him to the spot. Disbelief and a sudden, sharp rush of happiness hit him, something he hadn't felt in quite a while.

It was a text from Ella.

"Thanks for the money, Dad. The trip was fun."

Isaac's thumb hovered over the keyboard. His chest felt tight, but in a good way, like a knot loosening after years of tension. Part of him wanted to overthink it, to write something clever, something measured. But another, louder part of him, the part that had spent the morning kneeling in the parking lot and walking to the front of the church, told him to just say it. Just be honest.

"I'm glad. I love you."

As he typed the words, a warmth spread through his chest, slow and steady, surprising in its intensity. He exhaled quietly, pressed send, and sat back for a moment, letting the words linger between him and her across the miles.

Isaac got home, his apartment calm and clean. He took down his long-forgotten Bible, opened it at random, and landed on Psalms forty-six.

God is our refuge and strength, a very present help in trouble.

He read it again, letting the words sink in. When he reached *"Be still, and know that I am God,"* he closed the Bible, heart lighter than it had been in years. The quiet wasn't empty; it was a gift. For the first time, Isaac felt truly seen, truly anchored, and not alone.

Sit with Isaac's story, not as entertainment, not as inspiration, but as a mirror. How is your mind right now? Ordered or chaotic, clear or cluttered? Can you hear God through the noise, or has it become indistinguishable from your own anxious thoughts? Isaac didn't break down over something big. He broke down over a toaster, but the toaster was just a symptom of years spent trying to control what he couldn't while refusing to surrender what he could. How many "toasters" are in your life? How long has it been since you felt really quiet, real stillness, real presence in your own life? Restoring your mind isn't optional; it's spiritual survival. Start small: make a list, admit you need help, clean your space, sit in silence. Don't wait. Be still. Know that He is God. Everything else is just noise.

CHAPTER 4:
SURRENDERING OUR LIVES TO GOD

"Trust in the Lord with all your heart and lean not on your own understanding; in all your ways acknowledge Him, and He shall direct your paths."
- Proverbs 3:5,6

Eve Foster had not cried in eleven years. She could pinpoint the exact moment it stopped, December seventh, a Thursday. The day she stood in front of her mother's casket and felt absolutely nothing. No grief. No loss. Not even the hollow imitation of sadness people perform at funerals. There was only a vast, echoing emptiness where emotions were supposed to live.

Her sister Rachel sobbed through the entire service, shoulders shaking, face buried in trembling hands. Her brother Peter delivered the eulogy with a voice that cracked and wavered, barely holding together long enough to finish. The extended family gathered close, offering comfort and sharing memories, their faces wet with tears and flushed with sorrow. And Eve stood among them, dry-eyed, distant, untouched, watching it all the way one watches a documentary about a stranger's family. Observant. Removed. Clinically detached. As if grief were something happening on a screen just out of reach, rather than a force meant to tear through her chest.

That was the day she understood something fundamental about herself. Emotions were a weakness. Tears were a sign of losing control, and control was the only thing that mattered in a world that was constantly trying to knock you flat. So, she stopped crying, she stopped allowing herself to feel anything too deeply, anything that might crack her open or leave her exposed. She built her walls, high, thick, and unforgiving, brick by careful brick. Nothing was allowed through them. Not joy. Not sorrow. Not love. Not pain. Behind those walls, she was safe.

Nothing. It had cost her nothing, at least not in ways the world could measure. Eve Foster was forty-one years old and the Chief Operating Officer of a pharmaceutical company generating three billion dollars in annual revenue. She oversaw operations across fourteen countries, managed a staff of four thousand, and made decisions every day that affected thousands of lives, millions of dollars, and entire markets.

She was exceptional at her job because she did not let feelings interfere with logic. Where other executives agonized over layoffs and restructuring, Eve made hard calls without hesitation. While her colleagues grew attached to projects or people, Eve stayed objective. Where sentiment clouded judgment, she operated with cold, precise clarity.

The board loved her for it. Shareholders trusted her for it. Quarterly earnings remained strong because Eve never allowed emotion to compromise efficiency.

She had been married once, a lifetime ago, to a man named Daniel, who had loved her with an earnest devotion that seemed charming in her twenties and suffocating by her thirties. He wanted children; she wanted a career. He dreamed of Sunday dinners and family vacations; she chased promotions and corner offices. He wanted her to feel things. She wanted him to stop asking her to.

The divorce had been civil. Efficient. She handled it the way she handled everything else, with minimal drama and maximum effectiveness. Daniel remarried within two years. He had three children now. Every Christmas, he sends a card with photos of his smiling family, images she glanced at once before throwing them away.

She didn't envy him. She didn't miss what they'd had. She had made her choice, and she was living with it. Some people were meant for families and feelings. Eve was meant for boardrooms and balance sheets. That was what she told herself. That was what she had believed for eleven years.

Until this morning, when her carefully controlled world began to show its first cracks.

It was 5:47 a.m. Eve was already at her desk in her home office, reviewing reports from the Asian markets that had closed hours earlier. A 7 a.m call with Europe. An eight-thirty meeting with her direct reports. A nine-thirty presentation to the board. Her day was mapped in fifteen-minute increments, every moment accounted for, every minute optimized.

Control. That was what made her dangerous in business.

She controlled her time, her emotions, her outcomes. She left nothing to chance. She prepared for every contingency, with backup plans for her backup plans. Her phone rang.

She answered without looking at the screen. "What is it?"

"Miss Foster," her assistant Peter said, not her brother, but just as meticulous, "I'm sorry to call before six, but we have a situation."

She was already pulling up the operations dashboard on her second monitor. "I see the alert. The Ohio facility. When did this happen?"

"About three hours ago. Power went down across the entire region, not just us. The whole grid."

"Cause?"

"That's the problem. They're calling it unprecedented. Every backup system failed at once. Even the diesel generators won't start. It's like… everything electronic just stopped."

Something fluttered in her chest. She ignored it.

"What's the estimated downtime?"

"We don't have one. The power company isn't responding, cell service is unstable, and…" He hesitated. "There's something else."

She exhaled slowly. "Go on."

"We've been monitoring social media and some news outlets. This isn't isolated to Ohio. There are reports of similar blackouts in Chicago, Detroit, and parts of Pennsylvania. All within the last week."

Eve's fingers stilled over the keyboard. "Correlation isn't causation."

"Yes, ma'am. But people are… saying things."

That earned a dry, incredulous laugh. "People always say things."

"They're claiming they heard something before the power went out. A sound. Like a trumpet." He lowered his voice, as if embarrassed. "And there are videos, empty clothes in the streets. Some outlets are calling it the Rapture."

Silence stretched. Then Eve laughed again, short, sharp, genuinely amused.

"The Rapture," she repeated. "Of course they are."

"I know it sounds irrational," Peter rushed on. "But there's a lot of chatter about biblical prophecy and end times, and I thought you should at least be aware of what's circulating."

She closed her eyes and took a measured breath. "Peter, when humans encounter an unexplained event, they reach for superstition because it's easier than uncertainty. Power grids fail. Sometimes multiple grids fail, solar activity, cyberattacks, and infrastructure decay. There are dozens of explanations that don't involve divine intervention."

"Yes, ma'am."

"What I need from you is facts, not internet hysteria. Contact the facility director. Get a full operational assessment. Identify which locations are affected and which aren't. Draft a communication plan for clients and shareholders."

"Understood."

"And Peter," she added coolly, "keep your head, this is a logistics problem, not a theological crisis."

"Yes, Miss Foster. I'll handle it immediately."

The line went dead. Eve turned back to her screens, the faint smile still lingering, utterly convinced the world, like everything else, could be managed.

She ended the call and leaned back in her leather chair. The flutter in her chest hadn't subsided. She dismissed it immediately. Emotions were nothing more than chemical reactions. Anxiety was just adrenaline misinterpreted by people who lacked discipline, a convenient excuse.

She spent the next hour proving it. Reports were pulled. Emails sent. Calls made. By seven a.m., she had a clear operational picture. Three manufacturing facilities were offline. Two distribution centers were unresponsive. The financial impact would be significant but manageable if power were restored within forty-eight hours. If not, contingency protocols would be implemented, and production would be shifted to unaffected sites. Simple. Contained.

Control. She was still in control.

The 7 a.m call with the European team went smoothly. By eight, Eve was dressed and ready. Her makeup routine followed the same sequence it had for years: cleanser, toner, moisturizer. Foundation applied evenly, blended without excess. Concealer where necessary. Neutral eyeshadow. One precise line of eyeliner. Mascara, two coats, no more. Blush, minimal. Lipstick in a muted, professional shade. Hair smoothed, parted, secured. No experimentation. No creativity. The goal was not beauty, only presentation. Pristine. Controlled.

She grabbed her bag and keys and walked into the garage, where her Tesla sat charging. She pressed the unlock button, but nothing happened. She pressed it again, still nothing.

She stepped closer and tried the driver's-side handle. The car was dead. The screen was black, and even the charging indicator was off. Yesterday it had functioned perfectly. Now it sat there like an eighty-thousand-dollar sculpture.

The flutter in her chest tightened into a clamp. This was fine; cars had electrical failures, and it was normal. She would call for service, take an Uber, and deal with it later.

She opened the Uber app anyway. It spun endlessly, searching, failing. She walked out into the driveway, lifted the phone higher, tried different angles, different spots in the yard. Nothing, the sensation in her chest sharpened, insistent now. Her pulse quickened; she refused to name it.

Anxiety was a story people told themselves when they didn't want to confront reality. It wasn't real. It was a weakness disguised as a diagnosis. She stood very still in her driveway, phone clenched in her hand, telling herself, firmly, that this was nothing more than an inconvenience.

The street was quiet, too quiet for an eight a.m morning on a weekday. Normally, there would be the low hum of departure: car doors slamming, engines turning over, children laughing too loudly while waiting for school buses, the soft chaos of a neighborhood waking itself up. This morning, there was nothing. No movement.

No voices. No cars. Every visible house sat still and closed, as if abandoned overnight.

Something shifted inside her. Something she had not allowed herself to feel in eleven years.

Fear.

Not the calculated concern she felt when a deal went sideways, not the analytical assessment of risk she lived on. This was different, primal. It rose from her gut and spread through her body like ice water in her veins, tightening her chest, hollowing her breath. A warning, ancient and unmistakable.

Something was wrong.

Not a power outage. Not a dead car. Not spotty cell service. Something larger, something her assistant's words had brushed against, and she had laughed away because to consider it would mean admitting she wasn't in control.

She backed into the house and tried the lights, but nothing. The television stayed black, she tried her laptop, it powered on, running on battery, but refused to connect to anything beyond itself. One by one, she checked every device, every system that depended on an external signal, a grid, a network, but it was useless, useless. The house was silent, dark, severed from the world.

She stood there, surrounded by stillness, and felt the foundations of her carefully constructed life begin to crumble.

This couldn't be happening. She planned for contingencies. She prepared for disruptions. She had emergency supplies in the basement. Cash in the safe. A full tank of gas in her second car, the old Honda she kept for utility, not status.

She went back to the garage and tried it. The engine turned over immediately, the sound solid and reassuring. Old mechanical engineering, no screens or silent failure, just pistons and fuel and motion. She slid into the driver's seat and gripped the steering wheel, her hands tighter than she realized, her breath shallow as she tried to decide what to do.

Going to work was the logical choice. Even without power, she could coordinate response efforts, gather people, and make decisions. Take control.

But something stopped her.

An invited memory rose from a place she had sealed off years ago. Her grandmother's kitchen, warm and dim, smelling of bread and old books. Sunday afternoons stretched long and slow. A woman who believed easily, gently, in a way Eve's parents never had. A woman who read Bible stories aloud, her voice soft but certain, as if she were describing things she *knew* were true.

"Jesus will come back one day," her grandmother used to say, smoothing Eve's hair as she sat cross-legged on the floor. "And when He does, it'll be quick."

Eve had believed her then. Completely. As children do. She remembered asking questions, wide-eyed, earnest.

"How will we know?"

Her grandmother had smiled softly. "You won't get a warning, child. That's why you don't wait to get ready."

"Ready for what?"

"For Him," she'd said, tapping Eve gently on the chest. "For the trumpet. For the moment. You have to be ready *before* it happens, because you don't know the day or the hour."

That certainty had comforted her once. The idea that the world had an order. An ending that meant something.

But adulthood had burned that out of her. The more Eve learned about markets, systems, politics, and power, the less room there was for faith. Reality was brutal and random and uninterested in belief. Religion became something else in her mind: a coping mechanism, a way people softened chaos so they could sleep at night. Her grandmother had been kind and loving, but she was naïve. Eve had outgrown that softness.

Now, sitting alone in her driveway, the engine idling, Eve heard that voice as clearly as if her grandmother were beside her.

"When the trumpet sounds," the voice said gently, "there won't be time to run around fixing things. You have to be ready already."

"No," Eve whispered, shaking her head. She gripped the steering wheel harder, as if she could physically push the memory away. This was a shock. Stress. An overactive imagination grasping for meaning where none existed. There was a rational explanation for this; there had to be. Power grids failed. Networks collapsed. Systems broke.

Faith didn't suddenly become real because the lights went out.

She backed out of the driveway and drove. Street after street passed in silence. Cars sat neatly in driveways, untouched. No people. No movement. When she reached the main road, her stomach dropped. It was just as empty. No traffic. No honking. No distant sirens. Just her old Honda moving through a world that seemed to have paused mid-breath.

Her hands began to shake on the wheel. Her breath shortened. Not panic, but something close. She drove faster.

The closer she got to the city, the worse it became. Cars are abandoned everywhere. Some crumpled together at intersections. Others idled in lanes, doors ajar, as if their drivers had simply stepped out and never returned.

Then she saw the clothes, piled on sidewalks and slumped in car seats. Folded unnaturally on park benches. Shirts, shoes, and dresses were empty as if the people inside them had been erased.

Just like Peter had said. Just like the rumors she had laughed at online. Clickbait hysteria. Religious nonsense dressed up as breaking news.

Just like the rapture.

"No," she said aloud, louder this time. "That's not possible."

Eve pulled into the parking garage of her office building. Darkness greeted her, heavier than usual. The automated gate was stuck open, a silent invitation, or a warning. She parked the Honda and took the stairs, twelve flights up to the lobby level. Each step echoed in the empty building, and by the time she reached her floor, her breath was ragged, not from exertion, but from the crushing weight of the impossible reality pressing down on her.

The floor was dark. Emergency lights cast a dim, flickering glow across empty corridors. No security guards. No maintenance staff. No one. She moved toward the window, the city spread below her, a vast grid of silent streets. Chicago was dark, not just without electricity, but devoid of life. Smoke curled from fires that no one was fighting. Car alarms wailed intermittently, mechanical cries abandoned by human hands.

Eve pressed her palms against the glass, feeling a shudder rise from her chest. Control, the armor she had spent forty-one years forging…crumbled. The certainty that she could manage anything through logic and precision was shattered. And with its collapse came everything she had buried, every suppressed fear, every unclaimed longing, every lonely ache she had denied for over a decade.

She sank to her knees on the cold floor, the vast emptiness of the city mirrored in her own hollow chest. The sobs came without permission, violent and unrelenting, wracking her body. She cried for her mother, for the funeral she had attended with dry eyes, for the marriage she had ended because feelings were inconvenient, for the siblings she had kept at arm's length, for the friends and relationships sacrificed on the altar of control. She cried for the children she would never have, for the life she had meticulously designed to avoid chaos, and for the years spent convincing herself that surrender was weakness.

Time passed without measure. The sun moved across the sky, shadows shifting across her office, but she stayed there, absorbed in her grief. And as the storm within her began to ebb, exhaustion replaced panic. Her body felt hollowed out, empty. Every ounce of control, every carefully calculated choice, had poured out of her, leaving space, vacant, aching space.

And then the voice came back, soft and clear, carrying across decades: her grandmother's words from a summer evening when Eve had been eight.

"Child," she had said, rocking gently on the porch, "you're going to spend your whole life trying to be strong enough to handle everything on your own. You'll be smart. You'll be capable. You'll build a life that looks successful from the outside. But there will come a day when the weight is too heavy, when control is too exhausting, and you'll want to give up. When that day comes, know this: you're never meant to carry it alone. God didn't make you to be your own savior. You were made to surrender. And surrender isn't weakness, baby. It's the bravest thing you'll ever do."

Eve had rolled her eyes at the time. Surrender had seemed like giving up, a luxury for the weak. But now, in the darkened office with the abandoned city below, she understood. Surrender wasn't weakness. It was the only honest response to reality. She had spent her life believing she was in control, managing outcomes and manipulating circumstances, when in truth, the things that mattered, life, death, love, loss had never been hers to command.

And now, finally, she allowed herself to let go. To cry. To acknowledge that she could not, would not, carry this alone. The sobs came again, quieter this time, a rhythm of release. She pressed her hands to her face, feeling hollow, exhausted, terrified, yet somehow alive in the acknowledgment of her vulnerability. The truth was clear: control had always been an illusion, and for the first time, she was willing to surrender.

Eve pulled herself to her feet, her legs trembling beneath her as if they no longer fully trusted her. The strength was still there; she had never been weak, but it wavered now, unsteady in a way she had never allowed before. She crossed the office slowly, heels clicking too loudly in the space, and stopped at the window. The glass was cold beneath her fingertips as she looked out over the city once more.

Chicago lay beneath her like a body after death. Streets stretched out in perfect grids, dark and lifeless. Smoke drifted upward in thin, lazy columns from fires no one was tending. There were no headlights, no movement, no sound of voices rising from the streets below. Somewhere out there, maybe, there were others like her, people left behind, people who had believed themselves self-sufficient, people who had trusted their own strength until the moment it was stripped away. Or maybe she was alone. Maybe she was the only one standing in a world that had moved on without her.

It didn't matter.

Whether she was one among millions or utterly alone, the truth remained the same. There was nothing left to plan. Nothing left to manage. Nothing left to control.

The realization settled into her bones with a terrifying clarity. This was the moment her grandmother had warned her about, not with fear, but with certainty. Not later. Not once did she understand more. Not once had she gathered information or devised a strategy. Now. Right now. Total and irrevocable surrender.

Everything she had clung to for forty-one years loosened its grip at once. Her career. Her discipline. Her relentless competence. The belief that she could outthink, outwork, outlast anything life placed in front of her. It all slipped through her fingers, and for the first time, she did not try to grab it back. She didn't know how to pray.

Her grandmother had tried once, kneeling beside her bed when Eve was a child, hands folded, voice gentle—Eve had never listened. Words, posture, ritual, it had all seemed unnecessary, even foolish. Now, standing alone in her dark office with the city silent below her, she understood that God didn't need polished words. He didn't need the right form. He needed truth.

Eve sank to her knees again, not collapsing this time, but lowering herself deliberately. Her suit was wrinkled, her hair disheveled, her face streaked with dried tears. She looked nothing like the woman who had walked into this building that morning. She bowed her head, her hands resting uselessly in her lap, and spoke into the stillness.

"I can't do this."

The words were barely louder than a breath, but they felt like they tore something open inside her.

"I thought I could. I really did. I thought if I worked harder, planned better, stayed disciplined enough, I could handle anything. I thought strength meant never needing help." Her voice shook now, uneven, stripped of all polish. "But I can't handle this. I can't control it. I don't even understand it."

Tears spilled over again, hot and relentless, soaking into the carpet beneath her knees.

"I'm terrified," she whispered. "I'm terrified that I missed it. That I was so busy being in control that I missed the only thing that mattered. That I missed you."

Her throat closed around the word. She pressed her forehead to the floor, her body folding in on itself, small and unguarded.

"I don't know if you're listening. I don't know if there's mercy left for someone who spent her entire life refusing to need You." Her voice broke completely now. "But I'm asking anyway. I'm begging. Please hear me. Please see me. Please don't let this be the end."

She inhaled sharply, every breath a surrender.

"I give it to you. All of it. My career. My control. My pride. The life I built without You. I can't carry it anymore. I don't want to carry it anymore. I need you to carry it. I need you to carry me."

Her hands curled into the carpet as if anchoring herself.

"God… I surrender."

The words hung in the air, fragile and exposed. Eve waited. For warmth. For reassurance. For some unmistakable sign that she had been heard. Nothing happened.

The silence pressed in around her again, and panic flickered at the edges of her mind. Had she waited too long? Had she said it wrong? Was this what it felt like to reach out and find nothing there?

Then, quietly, almost imperceptibly, something shifted. Not in the room, in her.

It was small, like a door opening somewhere deep inside her, a door she had forgotten existed because it had been locked for so long. The fear didn't vanish. The uncertainty didn't lift. But beneath it all came something steady, something inexplicable.

Peace.

Not control. Never again. But peace that didn't depend on answers or outcomes. Peace that existed alongside terror. Peace that could not have come from within her because she had emptied herself.

She remained on her knees, but not in collapse now. In stillness. In something that felt like reverence. Like rest. Like finally allowing herself to be held.

She didn't know what came next. She didn't know if she had been saved or condemned, if her prayer had arrived in time or too late. She only knew that she had done the one thing she had spent her entire life refusing to do.

She had admitted she needed help.

The afternoon sun streamed through the office windows, casting long bands of light across the floor. Eve stayed where she was, with no plan, no next steps, no illusion of control. For the first time in her adult life, she had nothing figured out and somehow, astonishingly, that was okay.

The silence in the office remained, but it had changed. It no longer felt empty or oppressive. It felt like waiting, like breath held before something begins.

Eve lifted her head, her face swollen and tear-streaked, her eyes red and raw. She felt unmoored, uncertain, like someone who had been gripping the edge of a cliff for years and had finally let go. But beneath that uncertainty was a strange sense of freedom, like a boat released from its moorings after being tied too tightly for too long, finally allowed to drift on currents it did not control.

Eve stepped out of her office building, the cool evening air brushing against her cheeks. The city was still, silent, and empty, but it no longer felt hostile. It no longer felt like a testament to her failure. Now it was simply reality, truth laid bare. She walked without direction, letting her feet guide her as her mind finally quieted. The streets of Chicago were littered with abandoned cars, clothes scattered like echoes of lives interrupted mid-moment. Shoes splayed on sidewalks, jackets draped across benches, a scarf fluttering against a lamppost in the faint breeze. Each fragment told a story she could not fix, a life she could not control, a human heartbeat she had never paused to consider.

For the first time, her sorrow was not about her own losses or the paths she had missed. It was for them, all these souls frozen in absence, all the lives swept away in a moment. She whispered into the fading light, words she had never mastered: "Please… let them have been ready. Please… let them have surrendered. Please… let them have said yes." The words felt clumsy, inadequate, but somehow enough. She did not know how to pray properly, but honesty had a power she had never felt in spreadsheets, schedules, or strategy.

As the sun dipped low, casting long amber shadows, Eve found herself standing in front of a small church, older than the towers that now loomed over the empty streets. Its wooden doors, simple and unassuming, were unlocked. She pushed one open and entered. The sanctuary smelled faintly of polished wood and incense long burned away. The light filtering through the stained glass painted soft, fractured colors across the worn pews and the stone floor. A simple cross hung on the wall, two pieces of wood intersecting, humble and unwavering in its quiet authority.

Eve moved slowly to the front, each step echoing softly in the emptiness, and lowered herself into the first pew. Her eyes rested on the cross, and for the first time, she truly understood what surrender meant. Jesus had surrendered, fully, utterly, without holding back. He had handed over His life to the Father, knowing the path would lead to suffering, to abandonment, to a cross and a tomb, and yet He trusted. He had relinquished control, and in three days, the tomb had been empty. She did not know if she had three days or three hours, but the principle was clear: surrender was not about securing a good outcome. Surrender was acknowledging who was truly in charge and stepping aside.

She bowed her head, her hands trembling as they rested on the pew before her. "I don't know what happens now," she whispered. "I don't know if it's too late, or if there's still time, or even what any of this means. But I'm done trying to figure it out. I'm done trying to control it. It's Yours. My life is Yours. Whatever that means. Whatever it costs. I'm Yours."

The words came out slowly, final, irrevocable. They hung in the dim light like smoke, rising and dissipating into the stillness of the sanctuary. No voice answered. No angel appeared. No divine hand reached down to guide her. Only silence. Only shadow. Only the cross, steadfast above her. And yet, when she finally lifted her head and stood to leave, she felt lighter. The weight she had carried for forty-one years, unacknowledged, unbearable, was gone. She could breathe fully for the first time in decades.

Outside, the streets were dangerous, cloaked in darkness, with no law, no lights, no order. Yet Eve felt no fear. Not because she could control what lay ahead, but because she had finally learned the secret her grandmother had tried to teach her. She was not meant to handle it alone. She was meant to trust the One who could.

Eve returned to her car, drove home through the silent city, and stepped into her dark house. She lit candles, ate simply from her pantry, and when night fell, she climbed into bed. Surrounded by uncertainty, she did something she had not done since childhood—she prayed herself to sleep. Not with rehearsed words or theological precision, but with honest, trembling conversation:

"Thank you for catching me. Thank You for not giving up on me, even when I gave up on You. Help me tomorrow. Teach me surrender, day by day. Show me how to live without control. I don't know how to do this… but I trust you."

Sleep came swiftly, untroubled, unbroken. The first peaceful rest in eleven years.

When morning arrived, she rose into a changed world, yet she walked without the crushing weight of needing to have everything figured out. Without the burden of being her own savior. For the first time, she woke surrendered, and that surrender, the quiet turning over of everything she had tried to carry herself, was the beginning of her real life. The life she had been created for all along.

Eve had spent forty-one years building her life on self-sufficiency, brilliant, disciplined, successful by every measure the world values. But when the trumpet sounded, the world shifted, and her carefully laid plans failed; she discovered she had nothing. She had prepared for everything except surrender, fortified everything except her soul. Standing alone in an empty office, tears streaming, she finally spoke the words she had resisted all her life: "I can't do this. I need you. I surrender." In that moment, the weight she had carried for decades lifted, and for the first time, peace arrived, not control, not answers, not certainty, but the steady relief of letting go.

This is the mirror her story holds for every life built on pride and self-reliance. You cannot carry it all alone. You were never meant to. Every day spent proving otherwise is a day built on sand. Surrender now, your career, your control, your carefully managed life, the illusion that you are in charge. Lay it down. Give it to God. Let Him carry what you were never meant to carry. Freedom, relief, and true life are found not in holding on, but in letting go.

CHAPTER 5:
MIRROR TO THE SOUL

"Anyone who listens to the word but does not do what it says is like someone who looks at his face in a mirror and, after looking at himself, goes away and immediately forgets what he looks like. But whoever looks intently into the perfect law that gives freedom, and continues in it—not forgetting what they have heard, but doing it—they will be blessed in what they do."
- James 1:23-25

The sanctuary was already warm when Jacob stepped behind the pulpit, sunlight filtering through the tall stained-glass windows and breaking into soft colors that pooled across the pews, blues and ambers washing over familiar faces turned toward him with expectation, with trust, with the quiet hunger of people who believed he had something to give them. The choir had just finished the final note of the opening hymn, voices lingering in the air like a held breath, and Jacob rested his hands on the worn wood of the lectern, feeling the grooves his fingers had carved there over the years, a physical record of sermons preached and prayers offered, of words spoken so often they had become muscle memory.

"Good morning," he said, his voice steady, warm, practiced to perfection, and the response came back exactly as it always did, a unified chorus of "Good morning, Pastor", smiles spreading, heads nodding, notebooks opening, pens poised as if revelation were already descending. He smiled back, the expression appearing on his face without effort, without thought, as natural as breathing, and

launched into the sermon with the ease of a man who had told this
story a hundred times before.

"We talk a lot about faith," he continued, pacing just slightly
now, the way he knew worked, the way that kept eyes following him,
"but faith isn't just about what we say we believe, it's about what we
live when no one else is watching," and a murmur of agreement
rippled through the room, a few *amens* rising from the front pews,
right on cue.

Jacob heard his own words as if they belonged to someone else,
each sentence arriving polished and complete, illustrations dropping
into place at the exact moments they were supposed to, Scripture
quoted smoothly, pauses timed for emphasis, laughter landing where
it always landed, and all the while something inside him remained
utterly untouched. He watched the congregation lean forward,
watched a young couple clasp hands, watched an older woman dab
at her eyes with a tissue, watched a man in the third-row nod
vigorously as if every word were striking deep into his soul, and felt
a strange, distant awareness that they were receiving something real,
something meaningful, even as he himself felt nothing at all.

He spoke about honesty before God, about laying down masks,
about the danger of living a double life, and the irony brushed against
him so lightly it barely registered anymore, because he had been
doing this long enough now to know exactly how to sell sincerity
without ever feeling it. His mouth moved, his hands gestured, his
voice softened and rose in all the right places, but his mind drifted
just beyond the sound of his own speech, struggling to stay tethered
to the present, struggling even to listen to himself as the words
poured out, fluent and hollow.

There had been a time, he knew, when these sermons had come
from somewhere deeper, when he had stood in this same space and
felt conviction burn in his chest, when the words had first passed
through him before reaching anyone else, but that time felt distant
now, blurred, as a memory recalled too often to trust. Pretending
had started subtly, almost kindly, just pushing through exhaustion,
just doing what needed to be done for the sake of the people, and

somewhere along the way, the pretending had become seamless, effortless, so convincing that even he had nearly believed it.

"As we go into this week," Jacob said, his voice gentle now, reverent, "I want you to remember that God desires your truth, not your perfection," and the congregation responded again, voices overlapping, faith blooming visibly in their expressions, while Jacob stood there thinking only of how strange it was that they could take every word to heart while he stood behind the pulpit feeling like a spectator to his own performance, delivering lines he had memorized long ago, waiting for the final *amen* so he could step down, smile, shake hands, and continue pretending just a little longer.

The next morning, Jacob woke before the alarm, as he often did, to the low hum of traffic outside and the stale quiet of his apartment. The place always felt dim, even in daylight, with heavy curtains, neutral walls, and furniture chosen for function rather than comfort. He sat on the edge of the bed for a moment longer than necessary, shoulders slumped, joints stiff, the weight of another day already pressing down on him. In the bathroom, he turned on the tap and let the water run, splashing his face, keeping his eyes deliberately lowered as he reached for his toothbrush. He focused on the sink, the counter, the small crack in the tile near the drain, anywhere but the mirror. Looking would require reckoning. And Jacob Darty had mastered the art of avoidance.

Jacob Darty had not looked at himself, really looked at himself, in three years. He saw his reflection every day, of course, in bathroom mirrors while brushing his teeth, in shop windows while walking to work, in the rearview mirror of his car, but he didn't look or meet his own eyes. He skimmed past his reflection the way you skim past a stranger on the street, acknowledging the presence without engaging with the person. Because if he really looked, he'd have to see what he had become, and he wasn't ready for that. He was fifty-one years old, a pastor, with twenty-three years in ministry for twenty-three years. He led a congregation of four hundred people at Cathedral of Love Missionary Baptist Church.

The power was out, that was his first thought when his alarm didn't sound, and he opened his eyes to a bedroom darker than it should have been at six-thirty in the morning. Another outage, he assumed, another one in a growing pattern, rolling blackouts, infrastructure problems, a utility company full of apologies and empty promises. But when Jacob got out of bed and looked through the window, his chest tightened. The entire neighborhood was dark, every house unlit, no streetlamps, no distant glow from the city, just a hollow stretch of shadow where normal life should have been.

And it was quiet, profoundly so, the kind of quiet that felt unnatural in a world always humming with machines. He reached for his phone. Dead. Not drained, not sleeping, dead in a way that suggested it would never turn on again. He tried the light switch, then another, then another as he moved through the house, each click met with nothing, and as the silence pressed in around him, Jacob felt the unsettling sense that this wasn't just a power outage, but the absence of something deeper, something the world had quietly taken with it.

Martha was already awake, standing in the kitchen with a single candle cupped in her hand, its flame casting uneven light over the countertops and the useless appliances that lined them. She was still beautiful to Jacob in the way only someone who had shared his life for decades could be, her face familiar down to the smallest details, though the glow that once lived so easily in her had thinned, worn down by years of quiet strain. Her hair was pulled back loosely, the way she always wore it at home, and in the candlelight, the lines around her eyes looked deeper, not simply from age, but from carrying more than she ever said out loud.

"How long has it been out?" he asked, stepping closer without thinking, close enough to feel her warmth.

"I don't know," she said. "It was out when I woke up. Five." She turned then, and the look she gave him was one he had seen a thousand times in their marriage, equal parts fatigue and unspoken expectation.

"When was the last time you checked on the neighbors next door?" she asked.

"Yesterday," Jacob said. "Why?"

"I knocked on their door about ten minutes ago," Martha said, lowering her voice as if the house itself might be listening. "No one answered. Their car's still in the driveway, Jacob, but the house feels empty." She shook her head slightly. "I can't explain it. It just feels wrong."

Something cold moved through Jacob's chest he had heard the rumors, of course, everyone had by now, the stories that had been circulating for weeks about cities going dark without warning, about a low, unplaceable sound some people swore they'd heard just before everything stopped, about piles of clothing left on sidewalks with no bodies to account for them, about the rapture whispered in half-joking voices that never quite sounded like jokes. Jacob had dismissed it all from the pulpit the previous Sunday, not angrily, not defensively, but with the steady calm of a pastor who understood the danger of letting fear masquerade as faith, preaching instead about staying grounded, about refusing to be distracted by speculation and hysteria, about wisdom and discernment in an age where misinformation spread faster than truth.

He had been convincing, convincing enough that even he had believed himself.

"I'm sure they're fine," Jacob said now, though the words felt thin as they left his mouth. "Maybe they left early. Maybe they're visiting family."

Martha didn't answer right away. She looked at him the way she did when she already knew he was wrong.

"Their car is still there," she said quietly. "You know that."

He swallowed. "Cars get left behind all the time."

"And it's not just them, Jacob." Her voice dropped, the candle trembling slightly in her hand. "I walked down the street before you woke up. Every house feels empty. I don't mean quiet. I mean empty." She shook her head, a small, unsettled motion. "I can't explain how I know, but I know. Something's happened."

Jacob forced a breath, the practiced calm sliding back into place like a well-worn robe. "People are scared," he said. "Fear makes us imagine patterns that aren't there. It's how rumors turn into panic."

"They're gone," Martha said, more firmly now. "People are gone."

Jacob wanted to argue, wanted to explain why that couldn't be true, wanted to slip back into the familiar role of certainty and soothe his wife with measured reasoning and practiced calm. He wanted to sound like a pastor again, grounded and unshaken, offering explanations that made the world feel orderly and intact. But he couldn't, because beneath the instinct to reassure, he felt it too, the emptiness, the absence, the wrongness of the air itself, as if something essential had been quietly removed while the world slept, leaving behind a hollow version of reality, and Jacob knew with a growing, unnamable fear that the life he had gone to bed believing in no longer existed in quite the same way when he opened his eyes.

"I… I need to get to church," Jacob said, forcing the words out. "Check on people. Make sure they're… okay."

Martha nodded, but her eyes didn't lie. She knew. She knew he wasn't really going to check on anyone. He was running from this moment, from the thought that maybe the rumors weren't rumors, that maybe last Sunday he'd led his flock away from the truth instead of toward it.

"Can you stay here?" he added. "Keep trying the neighbors?"

"I'll try," she said, her voice soft, wary.

Jacob got dressed quickly, pulling on his dark suit, crisp white shirt, and black tie, the uniform of a pastor, each piece familiar, each adjustment a practiced ritual. He slipped on his polished shoes, feeling the tremor in his hands but ignoring it, running his fingers over the smooth leather as if that small contact could steady him.

His old pickup started, thank God, mechanical enough that whatever had killed the electronics hadn't touched it. He drove through the neighborhood in the pale early light. Martha was right. The houses weren't just quiet. They were empty, like a theater after the audience has left. A few cars were abandoned in the middle of the road, some crashed, some frozen as if the driver had vanished mid-commute. His hands shook on the wheel.

The church parking lot was empty. The building was dark. He let himself in through the side door, the one that still worked without electronics. Silence pressed in, echoing his footsteps down the hall to his office. He sank into the chair behind the desk where he had prepared thousands of sermons, counseled hundreds of people, prayed for guidance, and slowly became a stranger to himself.

Jacob let the dim light settle across the room and felt the weight of it all, the Sundays he'd preached about surrender while gripping the pulpit like a lifeline, the counseling sessions filled with advice about honesty while hiding his own fears, the prayers delivered to an audience while his own faith had quietly drained away. He'd become a professional Christian, fluent in ritual and language, polished in appearance, but somewhere along the way, the faith had leaked out, leaving only the performance.

He walked to the small bathroom attached to his office, the quiet of the church pressing around him like a held breath, he turned on the faucet, forgetting for a moment that nothing worked, and when the water came he remembered, the church had its own well, gravity-fed, the one piece of life here untouched by the blackout, the one thing that still obeyed natural law instead of electricity. He splashed the cold water over his face, the shock bringing him alive, but he didn't step back, didn't shy away. He made himself do what he hadn't done in three years. He looked up.

Into the mirror.

The face staring back was his own, unmistakable and yet strangely foreign. Fifty-one years carved into brown eyes, hair threaded with gray, a beard that had seen more winters than he cared to count. Lines etched around his eyes and mouth, earned in decades of smiling, comforting, speaking words that carried weight but were often hollow at the center. He studied them now, those lines, and felt them like cracks in a wall he had spent years pretending was whole.

His eyes, they were empty. Not dead, not cold, not cruel, just… empty. Like windows to a house where no one lived anymore. The lights were on, the furniture in place, the world functioning outwardly, but inside, no one remained. The performance continued, but the person behind it had slipped away.

Jacob gripped the edge of the sink, knuckles white, and forced himself to hold the gaze he had avoided for so long. He remembered being different once, messy, uncertain, alive. In his twenties, when the call to ministry first stirred in him, his faith had trembled and wrestled and burned with real need. He had prayed because he wanted God to answer him, not because it was scheduled or expected. Sermons had been born from struggle and questioning, not polished from a library of homiletics or the accumulated wisdom of decades spent pleasing an audience. He had been Jacob Darty then, flawed and human, reaching toward God with trembling hands and an open heart.

Now he was a pastor, yes, but not the same man. A professional Christian, fluent in ritual, polished in appearance, fluent in the language of comfort and guidance. A man who had learned, year by year, to value performance over presence, reputation over truth, applause over authenticity. The transition had been imperceptible, like the slow creep of time etching wrinkles he never noticed forming. Like a person gaining weight one meal at a time until one day nothing fits anymore. Only what had been compressed, reshaped, and squeezed until it no longer fit was his soul.

And he had let it happen. No, worse, he had built it, piece by piece, consciously, carefully, molding himself to the expectations of others until the man who had wrestled with scripture, who had trembled in prayer, who had once believed, was gone. He had chosen the mask over the man, the performance over the presence, the voice people needed to hear over the voice God had made him to be. And now, looking at his own reflection, he felt the weight of every Sunday he had preached without heart, every counseling session that had been a polished act, every prayer offered for show. The mirror held nothing back, and for the first time in years, Jacob felt the raw ache of being utterly, painfully human and utterly, painfully alone.

And now, looking at his own reflection, Jacob understood something with terrible clarity. He'd missed it. Whatever had happened in the night. Whatever the empty houses meant. Whatever the rapture was or wasn't. He hadn't missed it because he didn't know Jesus, or because he had never prayed, read the Bible, or given his life to God; he had done all that, meant it at the time, believed it as a teenager at church camp. But somewhere between that genuine surrender and this moment, he had taken his life back. He had made himself the center again, pushed God to the periphery, kept the vocabulary, the rituals, the appearances of faith, while letting the substance drain away.

He was a pastor who had forgotten how to pray. A shepherd who had lost sight of the Chief Shepherd. A man who spoke about God for a living but hadn't really talked to Him in years. The mirror began to fog with his breath, steam rising from the cold water splashed on his face. His reflection blurred, indistinct, as if he were disappearing. Jacob pressed his hand against the glass, leaving a print in the condensation, and through the fog, his eyes stared back at him, empty. The eyes of a man who had spent so long pretending to be found that he'd forgotten what being lost felt like. Until now.

"Who are you?" Jacob's voice cracked as he spoke the question aloud, echoing off the cold tile walls of the small bathroom. The sound was raw, unpracticed, nothing like the steady, confident voice he used from the pulpit, the one that inspired trust, the one that carried authority. "Who are you, Jacob Darty? Not who everyone thinks you are. Not who your congregation needs you to be. Who… who are you really?"

He leaned closer to the mirror, fog clinging to the glass, swirling around the outline of his face. Fifty-one years worn into his features, brown eyes rimmed with gray, hair-streaked silver, a beard carefully trimmed but soft now in the haze of steam. Lines cut around his eyes and mouth, the evidence of decades spent smiling, speaking, comforting, performing devotion he no longer felt. But it wasn't just the years on his face; it was the emptiness behind his eyes, the hollow center he could no longer deny.

The reflection didn't answer. It only stared back, unflinching, empty, and Jacob felt a tremor rise in his chest, a weight he had been holding down for years, decades even, buried under sermons, counseling sessions, prayers performed for show. And now it surfaced, insistent and raw: a scream, a protest, a desperate, inarticulate cry for the man he had lost.

The first sob escaped before he could stop it, heavy and ragged, tearing from deep in his chest. He gripped the edge of the sink, knuckles white, shoulders trembling as the heat of the shower mixed with his tears, steam curling around his face, blurring the reflection. He pressed his forehead to the glass, feeling his own breath fog it, watching his eyes, his real eyes, look back at him, raw, exposed, empty yet aching.

He let himself feel it fully, the truth he had spent years running from: he had lost himself. He had traded his soul for a successful ministry, for the approval of a congregation, for the appearance of devotion, for the comfort of being seen as a man of God. And now, staring at the man in the mirror, the man he had become, Jacob Darty realized that the cost had been everything: the heart, the fear, the doubt, the wrestling, the prayer, the surrender, all of it replaced with performance.

He sobbed harder, the sound filling the empty bathroom, his reflection trembling with him, and for the first time in years, he let himself feel the depth of his own failure, his own emptiness, his own loss, and he finally knew what it meant to be completely, painfully human.

And now the trumpet had sounded, or was about to, and Jacob Darty didn't know if he was ready. Didn't know if the professional version of faith he'd been performing was enough, or if God even recognized him anymore, when the man he had become bore so little resemblance to the man God had called. The bathroom was cold. The steam on the mirror was fading. His sobs quieted. He looked at the handprint on the glass, five fingers, a palm, the mark of a human being, a person, not a persona, not a performance. He wiped the mirror clear with his sleeve and looked again. His eyes were still empty, but now there was something else there, a faint recognition, the first stirring of someone waking from a long sleep.

Jacob spoke quietly this time. "Where did you go?" The question he had avoided for three years. Where had the real Jacob disappeared to? Was he still buried beneath the layers of pastoral performance, or had he been gone so long that nothing remained? His thoughts turned to his congregation, four hundred people who looked to him for guidance while he was spiritually lost. What had he given them? What had his sermons been worth when they came from emptiness? What good had his counseling done when he himself required counsel? He thought of last Sunday's sermon, when he'd dismissed the rapture rumors with confidence and authority. What if he had been wrong? What if his certainty had steered people away from preparing for the very thing that was now happening? What if his performance had cost more than just his own soul?

Jacob backed away from the mirror and turned from his reflection. He couldn't face what he saw, or what he didn't see. He walked out of the bathroom, through his office, down the hallway, and into the empty sanctuary.

Jacob stood in the center aisle of the empty sanctuary, his hands clutching the edges of the pulpit, knuckles white, nails digging into the polished wood as if gripping it could keep him upright. The stage lights above were dark, the windows letting in only the pale morning light, streaking the pews with ghostly lines. He swallowed, his throat tight, and his shoulders hunched, as though the weight of twenty-three years of sermons, smiles, and performances rested squarely on him.

"I don't know how to do this anymore," he whispered first, voice trembling, barely above the quiet echo of the empty room. He leaned forward, forehead almost touching the pulpit, his breath fogging the microphone, as if speaking closer would make the truth stick. "I don't know how to pray. I don't know how to lead. I've been faking it… every sermon, every counseling session, every prayer I've offered in front of people. I've been performing. For them. For me. For the image. And I've forgotten you."

His knees buckled, and he sank to the floor behind the pulpit, the wood scraping against his legs, sharp and grounding. He pressed his hands to the stage, fingers splayed, fingertips trembling as though they could feel the weight of the lies pressed into the floor. His forehead dropped to his palms, and his body shook, wracked with sobs he'd been holding in for years.

"I'm scared," he admitted aloud, voice breaking, rising and falling like a raw confession spilling from the deepest place he'd hidden. "I'm terrified, not of the world, but of what I've become. I've spent so long pretending, so long performing, that I don't even know who I am anymore. I don't know if there's anything left to save. But I'm telling you anyway. I'm laying it down. I'm lost. I'm broken. I'm scared. And I don't have a single answer."

He leaned forward further, forehead now pressed to the wood, tears streaking his face, dampening the collar of his shirt. The smell of polished wood and dust filled his nose. He lifted his head just enough for his eyes to meet the empty pews, trembling as if trying to project his confession into each empty seat. "I've led four hundred people while I was spiritually blind. I've preached about surrender while clutching my own reputation like it was life itself. I've taught about faith while forgetting to walk it myself. And I'm sorry. I don't know if it matters. I don't know if I've ruined it. But I'm telling you anyway. I'm confessing. I'm laying down the act. I can't do it anymore. I can't pretend."

His body slumped further, his spine curving, weight pressing into the floor, hands gripping the stage so tightly his knuckles ached. "Help me, God," he gasped, voice raw and wet with tears, shoulders shaking, back arching as though each word required every muscle to push through the fear and shame. "Help me find Jacob again, the messy, broken, real Jacob you called. Not the one I've made for everyone else. I'm here. I'm falling apart. I'm lost. But I'm here."

He collapsed fully onto his side, legs curled beneath him, face pressed into the wood, tears soaking the sleeve of his jacket. The sanctuary stayed silent, the echo of his voice fading, but the room didn't feel empty anymore; it felt alive with the weight of his honesty. And in that weight, Jacob felt a shift in himself, a small, fragile stir of something real. Not answers. Not peace. Just the awareness that he had spoken the truth aloud, that he had finally begun to find his way back from the performance, one trembling, broken confession at a time.

Jacob stood up, legs stiff and shaky, and walked back to the bathroom. The cool air brushed against his damp skin, carrying the faint scent of the polished wood from the pulpit. He stopped in front of the mirror and forced himself to hold his own gaze, refusing to look away.

The eyes staring back were still empty. Still lost. But now there was something else. Something small, fragile, almost imperceptible, a flicker. The first movement of life after a long sleep, a spark buried beneath years of performance and fear.

Jacob drove home through the steel-silent streets, the shadows of abandoned cars and darkened houses pressing in on him from all sides. His hands gripped the steering wheel so tightly it ached, knuckles white, shoulders tense, chest tight with a fear he couldn't name. By the time he reached their house, he felt hollow, drained, a man who had carried too much for too long.

Martha was waiting. She sat at the kitchen table, a single candle flickering between them, casting her face in trembling light and shadow. Her hair, once dark and lustrous, was streaked with gray; her eyes, lined with years of laughter and sorrow, seemed smaller somehow, dimmed. She wore a robe loosely tied, the kind of casual clothing that spoke of early mornings and long nights, of worry and waiting. She looked at him like she had been expecting him to fail, and in some deep part of her, she had known he already had.

"Did you find anyone?" she asked, voice small, tentative, as if speaking too loudly might shatter the fragile reality around them.

"No," he said, his own voice hoarse. "The church… it was empty."

She nodded slowly, as if that confirmed a fear she had already felt. Then, almost whispering, "I think they're gone, Jacob. I think the rapture… or whatever it is… I think we missed it."

He sank into the chair across from her, shoulders slumping, the weight of everything pressing him into the seat. The candlelight flickered over her face, and for a moment, he didn't recognize the woman in front of him. The woman he had married thirty years ago, the one whose laughter had once lit up every corner of his life, was both familiar and strange. She looked young and old at the same time, her beauty worn by time but still undeniable, her eyes carrying a fear and sadness he felt deep in his chest.

"I think you're right," he said finally, voice barely audible.

Tears welled in her eyes, spilling down her cheeks. "We are pastors, Jacob. How… how do we miss the rapture? How do we spend our lives in church, serving God, doing ministry, and miss the one thing that matters?"

He reached across the table and took her hands into his. His fingers trembled as they intertwined with hers, holding her in a way he hadn't in months, maybe years. The touch was raw, honest, grounding. "Because we got lost," he whispered. "Because we became professionals instead of disciples. Because we performed instead of surrendering. Because we were so busy doing church that we forgot about Jesus. I… I got lost, Martha. I'm so sorry. I should have been your spiritual leader. I should have been honest with you about how lost I was. I should have stepped down, or gotten help, or done something besides perform my way through it. But I didn't. And now… I don't know if we missed it, or if there's still time, or what any of this means. But I know I can't keep performing. I can't keep pretending. I have to be real now. Even if it's too late. Especially if it's too late. I have to be real."

Martha's hands squeezed his, tighter than before, trembling through his grip. Her tears fell freely now, wetting the candlelight with their sheen. "I knew," she said, voice breaking. "I knew you were lost. I could see it. But I didn't know how to reach you. I didn't know how to reach you when you were so busy being Pastor Jacob that there was no room for just... Jacob."

He bowed his head, voice raw and breaking, repeating the only words that seemed enough: "I'm sorry. I'm so sorry."

For a long moment, they sat like that, hands intertwined, bodies close, the candle flickering between them, tears running freely. Not the polished grief of a pastoral couple comforting each other. Not the controlled, quiet sorrow expected of people who are supposed to have it all together. But the raw, jagged, exposed grief of two souls realizing they had spent decades living parallel lives, caring for everyone but themselves, performing for everyone but each other.

Jacob finally lifted his head and looked at her, really looked, the flickering candlelight catching every line, every shadow, every glimmer of fear and love and longing in her face. Martha's shoulders shuddered with the force of her sobs. She pressed her forehead to his, the barrier of years of silence, pretense, and fear breaking in that small, intimate gesture.

After a long time, Martha spoke again. Her voice was small, fragile, like it might shatter if she pushed too hard. "What... do we do now?"

Jacob took a slow breath, letting it out in a shuddering sigh. His hands, still trembling from the drive, reached across the table. He took hers in a tentative handshake, fingers intertwining, grip hesitant at first, then firmer. The gesture was small, formal almost, but it carried weight, an unspoken promise of honesty, of presence, of reconnecting.

"We stopped performing," he said quietly, voice thick, gaze fixed on hers. "We stopped pretending. We look in the mirror and see who we really... actually are. And then... we ask God to help us become who we're supposed to be. Not who everyone thinks we are… who we're supposed to be."

Martha's eyes filled again, tears trembling at the edges. "Would that be enough? Will that fix this?"

He shook his head slowly, shoulders sagging, the tension of months and years of pretense pressing down on him. "I don't know. I don't think it's about fixing anything. I think… I think it's about being honest. About finally… after all these years of talking about surrender… actually surrendering. Not our time. Not our talents. Not our resources. But ourselves. Our real selves. The lost… the broken… the disappointing selves we've been hiding behind the pastoral persona."

Martha let that sink in. She leaned forward slightly, resting her elbows on the table, hands still wrapped in his, lips pressed tight. And then, finally, she said the words that broke him open and yet left a fragile thread of hope.

"I don't know who you are anymore, Jacob. And I don't think… I don't think you know who I am. We've been strangers… living in the same house… playing roles for each other the same way we play roles for the church."

He felt the words strike him like a hammer, chest tightening, eyes stinging. She was right. Completely right. The truth, spoken aloud, hurt so much it burned—and yet, it was liberating in its honesty. Jacob squeezed her hands, leaning forward to meet her gaze fully, as if physically bridging the years of distance between them.

"Then… let's meet each other again," he whispered, voice trembling. "Hi. I'm Jacob Darty. I am a pastor who's lost. A husband who's been absent. A man who's spent so long performing that he forgot how to be real. And I… I'm scared. Scared of what's happening in the world. Scared of who I've become. Scared that I've wasted years… trying to look spiritual instead of being spiritual."

Martha's tears fell freely now, streaking her cheeks, but a fragile, trembling smile broke through the pain for the first time in months.

"Hi," she said, voice raw. "I'm Martha Darty. I'm a pastor's wife who's been lonely… in a crowded church. A woman who's been playing the role of supportive spouse while dying inside… because my husband was too busy saving everyone else to notice I'm drowning. And I… I'm scared too. Scared we're too late. Scared we missed our chance. That we spent our lives doing all the right things… but missing the one thing that mattered."

Jacob nodded, feeling the weight of her truth press against his chest, their hands still entwined. Slowly, he squeezed hers, leaning just a little closer, letting his forehead brush hers. They stayed like that, hands clasped, faces close, trembling, tears falling freely. Not the polished grief of a pastoral couple comforting each other. Not the controlled sorrow expected of people who should have it together. But the raw, jagged, exposed grief of two souls realizing they had spent decades living parallel lives, performing for everyone but themselves, performing for each other but never truly connecting.

And in that seeing, something began to heal. Not the world. Not the circumstances. But something between them. Something that had been broken so long they'd forgotten it was supposed to be whole.

Jacob stood, slowly circling the table. Martha rose to meet him. They held each other, not the polite, practiced embrace of a pastoral couple, but the desperate, clinging hold of two people who had found each other again after being lost. Their bodies pressed close, hearts hammering in quiet rhythm, breaths mingling with the flickering candlelight, the shadows of the kitchen stretching long across the walls. Outside, the morning light grew, hesitant and pale, brushing across the floorboards. And there they were, finally real for each other, finally just themselves.

When they finally pulled apart, Jacob whispered, "I need to write a sermon."

Martha raised her eyebrows, voice trembling. "A sermon? For whom?"

"Everyone's gone," she said. "Maybe. But maybe there are others like us, others who've been left behind. Others who've been performing faith instead of living it. And if there's a Sunday, if there's any chance, I ever stand in that pulpit again, I need to say something different than I've ever said before." He spoke.

Jacob moved to his study, sat at his desk, and opened his journal, running. He began to write, not a polished sermon, not three points neatly arranged, not comforting clichés, but a confession. A mirror held up to himself, and to anyone else who had spent their life performing faith instead of living it.

The words poured out, raw, jagged, unpolished, alive with honesty.

"If you are reading this, stop. Stop pretending. Stop performing. Look in the mirror. See who you are. Really see. Not the version you show the world. Not the polished, approved, professional self. The one God actually made. The one you have been hiding from, even from yourself. Admit it. Admit that you are lost. That you are scared. That you have been faking. That your faith has sometimes been more about appearance than surrender. Admit it… and breathe.

Because here, in this confession, there is grace. Here, in this trembling honesty, there is a way forward. You do not have to be whole to start. You do not have to have it all together to speak to God. You do not have to be fearless to kneel. You only have to be real. Broken. Searching. Willing to admit you don't know. And that is enough. That is the first step toward being found.

I am Jacob Darty. Fifty-one years old. A pastor who has spent twenty-three years performing what I thought was faith, only to discover that the real thing was lost inside me. I am scared. I am lost. I am afraid I have failed those who looked to me. But I am here. I am alive. And I am willing to look. To feel. To surrender myself—not my sermons, not my reputation, not my image, but myself, completely, honestly, finally.

And if you are reading this, know this too: it is never too late to be real. To confess. To cry. To stumble, to fall, to get back up. To meet God where you actually are, not where you pretend to be. To see yourself. To see your neighbor. To be seen. That is where the kingdom begins, not in perfection, not in performance, but in the trembling, human, messy truth of who we are.

I need you to sit with Jacob's story. Jacob Darty spent twenty-three years performing faith, speaking eloquently from the pulpit while losing touch with the man he actually was, until the mirror finally forced him to see the stranger he had become. The trumpet has sounded; the empty streets and silent houses testify to a world moving on while he, and perhaps all of us, have been pretending. Don't wait for a crisis to confront yourself. Look in the mirror now. See who you are, not who you perform for, not who you wish you were, but who you actually are. Admit the truth. Feel the fear. Face the emptiness. Only there, in that honest, vulnerable, raw place, can transformation begin. The mirror is waiting. Your reflection is waiting. And time is running out.

CHAPTER 6:
BEARING THE FAULT

"The sacrifices of God are a broken spirit; a broken and contrite heart, O God, you will not despise."
- Psalms 51:17

Old man Phillips. That's what everyone called him, though I knew his name was Simon. A recluse, really, at least that's how the neighborhood framed him, a man who kept his curtains drawn and his mouth shut, which in a place like ours automatically made you suspicious. His house sat at the edge of the street like it had opted out of belonging, paint faded to something between white and surrender, porch boards that creaked even when no one was standing on them, wind chimes that only ever rang when the air turned sharp. His garden, though, was immaculate. Rows straight and deliberate, soil dark and cared for, vegetables growing as they trusted him completely, which should have told me something, but it didn't.

People talked. Not loudly. Not openly. The way people speak when they want to feel righteous without responsibility. Strange. Quiet. Keeps to himself. You know how it goes. I absorbed it all without questioning it, filed it away as discernment, and convinced myself I was seeing clearly when really, I was just seeing what was already there for me to see.

The package went missing on a Tuesday. Amazon said it delivered. Front door. Noon. I remember standing in my driveway, refreshing the tracking page, as if it might change its mind, as if truth could be negotiated. I checked the porch. The bushes. The side gate. Nothing.

And then I saw Simon across the street, kneeling in his garden, gloves on, back bent, entirely unbothered by my inconvenience. Something in me decided that was enough.

I told myself I was being practical. Logical. That it made sense. Who else would it be? I hadn't lost anything lately. I was organized. Responsible. The kind of man who notices details. The kind of man people trusted.

So, when I walked over to the mailbox later that afternoon and saw him there, sorting through envelopes slowly, I didn't hesitate. "Hey," I said, already tight, already certain. "You wouldn't happen to have seen a package delivered to my place, would you?"

He looked up, confused. "No."

"It says delivered," I replied, tapping my phone like it was scripture. "Someone must've picked it up by mistake."

His expression changed then, something closing. "I didn't take your package, Isaiah."

I smiled. That awful smile. The one meant to look gracious while cutting, anyway. "I'm just asking. No need to get defensive."

He held my gaze. "I'm not defensive. I'm telling you the truth."

But I'd already decided who he was. For the rest of the week, I punished him quietly with my looks and with my silence. The overly polite greetings sharpened with judgment. One morning, I even said it, the line that still makes my stomach turn. "Well, God sees everything," I told him, sweet as poison.

Then came the trunk.

I hadn't planned to clean it. I was just looking for jumper cables when I lifted an old blanket, and there it was. The box. Untouched. My name was printed clean and bold like an accusation I couldn't dodge.

I stood there longer than I want to admit. My chest is tight. My mind is scrambling for exits. Maybe it slid back here. Maybe someone moved it. Maybe this wasn't what it looked like. But it was. It was exactly what it looked like.

And suddenly the week replayed itself. His face. His voice. The way I'd enjoyed being right.

Walking to his house felt like walking toward myself without armor. Every step stripped something away. When he opened the door, rake in hand, dirt under his nails, he looked surprised but not guarded.

"I found the thief," I said, holding the box out between us. "It was me."

He stared at it. Then at me. Then he laughed. A real laugh. Loud enough to echo off the siding.

That was six years ago. And yet, the weight of it pressed on me this morning like a stone in my chest. The chipped ceramic mug warmed my hands, but it did little against the chill that had settled into my bones. The coffee burned my tongue, but it was bitter and flat, almost tasteless. Everything had lost its flavor. The silence of Lynwood clung to the streets like a shroud, heavy and unyielding, an absence where life used to hum. I could feel the memory of Simon pressing against me, sharp and accusing. I had been certain then, certain that he had wronged me, and I had judged him with all the fervor of a man who believed himself righteous.

I had leaned on certainty like a weapon, convinced I was right, and in that conviction, I had harmed. I hated myself for it. I hated the pride I had taken in my own discernment. I hated the way my conscience had remained silent while my ego ran unchecked. And even now, six years later, I could feel that old pattern lurking, the temptation to assume, to accuse, to find fault before knowing the truth. I knew that some mistakes live inside you longer than anyone else could ever measure, twisting themselves into your thoughts, into your heart, and all you can do is carry the shame and remember that once you are wrong in the life of another, the weight never fully leaves you.

It had happened just a few days ago, and I could still see it clearly when I closed my eyes. I had been drinking my morning coffee, the steam rising in slow spirals from my chipped mug, when I noticed movement in Simon's yard. At first, it was just a blur of color, the flash of a small boy running, his little legs pumping, arms flailing, tears streaking his face. I froze. My stomach clenched. Something about the way he ran, the way his cries tore through the quiet of the street, made my chest pound.

Then I saw Simon through the window, holding something long and shiny, a rod of some kind, and in that instant, I believed I was seeing what no one should ever see. The boy was screaming, running from Simon's side, and Simon didn't move to comfort him. My mind raced with images, assumptions, horror, and fear. I didn't think. I acted. I grabbed my phone and dialed 911, my voice shaking, urgent, spilling words I couldn't take back: "My neighbour… I think he's hurting a child… please, hurry."

I didn't stop to question, didn't wait to see the truth. I only saw what my panic painted. I watched through the window, wide-eyed, my chest tight, every second stretching like an eternity, until the boy reached his parents and they scooped him into their arms, whispering and shushing, holding him as he might crumble. And Simon, the rod still in his hand, wasn't doing what I had imagined. He wasn't harming the boy at all. He was cleaning a metal tool for his garden, something shiny he'd polished in the sunlight, the way he always tended his yard, and the boy had been running because he had scraped his knee the night before, and the parents had come outside to comfort him.

I felt my heart drop, my knees weaken. The phone was still in my hand. The cops were on their way. I could feel the guilt squeezing my chest, hot and sharp, and I wanted to scream into the empty street that I had been wrong, that I had seen monsters where there were none, that I had almost destroyed a man's life with my assumptions. I couldn't move, couldn't breathe properly, couldn't stop the memory of how quickly I had leapt into judgment, how eager I had been to accuse, how utterly human and shameful and fallible I was.

The police showed up faster than I expected, their cars crunching on the gravel of the street, lights muted in the pale morning, and I felt my chest tighten before I even stepped outside. Simon came to the door slowly, a hand pressed to the frame like he needed support, his face pale, eyes wide, and for the first time, I could see fear written clearly across him. Not the kind of fear that comes from guilt, but the kind that comes from being judged wrongly, from knowing the world is ready to believe the worst about you. He held the shiny rod loosely at his side, the same metal tool he had been polishing, and even that looked threatening to anyone who didn't know the truth.

The officers asked questions, their voices clipped, professional, but sharp enough to cut through the quiet of the neighborhood. Simon answered each one with a calmness that made my heart ache, but I could see how every word seemed to cost him something. He straightened his back, but only barely, and for a moment it looked like the weight of suspicion itself could make him crumble. I wanted to tell them he hadn't done anything, that I had been wrong, but the words felt useless in the face of what I had set in motion. The questions ended, they left their forms and warnings, and Simon shut the door slowly, leaning against it as if the walls themselves could hold him upright when his own strength faltered.

And the neighborhood didn't wait for the truth. Whispers started before lunch, voices slicing through yards and sidewalks, casual cruelty disguised as concern. "Did you hear about Phillips? Saw it all happen." "Poor kid, Phillips has always been… weird, you know?" "Can you believe someone like that would even live here?" Mothers whispered while children played too close to their homes, men nodded in the driveways, wagging their heads in judgment. I had handed them on a silver platter. I watched it unfold from my window, a horror that I had caused, and I felt the weight of every word, every suspicion, every sideways glance. Simon walked past the street the next day, eyes low, steps slow, like every footfall carried the burden of the lies I had lived in my own head.

It took me a day to find out the truth, though in those twenty-four hours,s I felt the weight of every whisper, every sideways glance, every judgment I had unleashed on Simon pressing down on me like a physical thing. I had gone over it again and again in my mind, imagining the worst, replaying the image of the boy running and Simon standing there with that shiny rod, feeling righteous in my own certainty. But when I finally saw the boy again, and I finally asked the parents, the truth came tumbling out in small, quiet sentences that landed in my chest like stones. The child, their grandson, had fallen in the yard, scraped his knee badly, and had been crying because it hurt, not because Simon had done anything to him. That shiny rod in Simon's hand had been nothing more than a metal stake he was cleaning for his garden, something he always polished in the sunlight before he used it to support his tomato plants.

The realization hit me harder than anything I could have imagined. I felt my stomach twist, my chest tighten, the air leaving me as if I had been holding my own punishment all along, and only now it had arrived. Every word I had said, every call I had made to the police, every whisper I had contributed to in the neighborhood, every judgment I had handed down like law, all of it had been wrong. Simon hadn't hurt anyone, hadn't threatened anyone, hadn't even raised his voice. He had simply existed, quietly tending to his garden, a man who lived his life carefully, and I had almost destroyed that with my panic, my assumptions, my failure to pause, to think, to see.

I couldn't stop shaking when I knocked on his door that evening. I didn't know if I could look him in the eye, if I could even say the words. But when Simon opened the door, he didn't accuse me, didn't yell, didn't demand an explanation. He simply looked at me, and in his expression I could see a mixture of disappointment, relief, and exhaustion, the kind that comes from being wronged and yet having the grace to survive it. I stammered something about being mistaken, about misunderstanding, about panic, but none of it felt enough. I felt smaller than I had ever felt in my life, my certainty stripped away, my pride crumbled into dust.

The next few days, I couldn't escape it. I watched from my window as the neighborhood whispered, judged, and stared at Simon like he had done something unforgivable, and I could feel it in my chest, in my gut, a slow, relentless burn that wouldn't let me rest. People crossed the street when they saw him, voices dropping when he walked past, small groups freezing mid-conversation as if they were afraid he might hear the unkind things they were saying. Children pointed, adults shook their heads in quiet condemnation, neighbors exchanged glances of disbelief, all of it swirling around him like a storm he had done nothing to summon. And I knew, painfully, that I had been the lightning rod, the spark that had set it all in motion, that my fear, my assumptions, my impulsive call to the police had turned him into something smaller than he was, something everyone else thought they understood but no one had ever known.

The guilt didn't wait for quiet moments; it followed me everywhere. In my bed at night, in the kitchen in the morning, even as I walked the streets pretending to do nothing wrong, it pressed on me, a constant weight, gnawing at me from the inside. I felt it in my hands, in the tightening of my chest, in the hollow taste of coffee, in the way every sound in the neighborhood seemed sharper, accusatory, as if the world itself was reminding me of the damage I had caused. I replayed the scene over and over, each time noticing new details I had missed before, every nuance of Simon's expression, every flicker of fear in his eyes, the way the boy ran, the way the parents embraced him, the way the shiny rod had glinted in the sun but had never been a weapon. And with each repetition, the shame grew heavier, the knowledge that I had almost destroyed a man's life with nothing but imagination and panic, and that everyone around him had believed it, had treated him as though he were guilty of some unspeakable crime, and that I had been the one to hand them that belief like a gift.

I couldn't speak to anyone without feeling it, without imagining that every word I said carried the weight of my mistake. I could feel my own judgment turning back on me, consuming me, reminding me how easily I had been wrong, how easily I had allowed certainty to masquerade as truth. And the more I thought about it, the more I understood how fragile trust is, how easily it can be shattered, and how a single misstep, my misstep, could echo through a life, through a neighborhood, through years of careful existence, leaving scars I couldn't see but could feel every time I looked at Simon walking past, quiet, stooped, carrying the burden I had created.

I stood at the edge of Simon's yard for longer than I wanted to admit, my feet rooted to the cracked sidewalk, my chest tight, my stomach twisting like a living thing. Each step forward felt heavier than the last, the air thick and silent, the neighborhood eerily empty after three days of blackout, and I felt exposed, like everyone who had whispered, who had judged, who had believed me was watching from their windows. My hands shook despite my best efforts to keep them still, my throat felt raw, and I could taste the coppery tang of fear with every shallow breath. I rehearsed the words over and over in my mind, but they sounded hollow, inadequate, powerless against the years of damage I had caused. I wanted to turn back, run to the safety of my own house, but something deep inside me—shame, perhaps, or the fragile hope that I could make this right- kept my feet moving forward, one trembling step at a time.

When I finally reached the porch, Simon was already there, adjusting the lens of his telescope, the polished metal glinting faintly in the pale morning light. He didn't turn immediately. When he did, his eyes found mine, calm, steady, and piercing in a way that made me want to disappear.

"Isaiah," he said, his voice raspy from disuse, carrying a weight I hadn't expected. "I've been expecting you."

My throat tightened, and for a moment I couldn't speak. The words I had rehearsed fell away, leaving only the raw ache of regret.

"You… you called the cops on me," he continued, his lips twisting slightly in disgust. "Said I was behaving suspiciously. That I had a weapon…" He gestured toward the shiny telescope at his side. "This," he said, voice tight, "is how I observe the heavens. Meteor showers, planetary movements. A lifelong hobby. Nothing else. Nothing you imagined."

The shame that washed over me in that instant was overwhelming. I felt smaller than I had ever felt, like I could melt into the wood of the porch or sink into the earth beneath my feet. My chest ached, my hands trembled, and I swallowed hard, forcing the words out.

"I was wrong," I said, barely above a whisper.

The confession hung between us, fragile and raw, the morning air heavy with it. For a brief moment, a flicker of something like forgiveness crossed his face.

"Yes," he said finally. "You are. Admitting you're wrong… It's a difficult thing. Most people aren't willing to do it, even when it's staring them in the face." He glanced back up at the telescope, his hands steadying the lens. "We are all operating on fear," he added softly. "Fear is a powerful motivator. It makes us see shadows where there is only light."

"I allowed my fear to cloud my judgment," I admitted, the words coming more easily now, flowing from a place of humility I hadn't known I still had. "I was wrong to accuse you as I did all those years ago. I offer my sincere apology."

He finally looked at me fully, his blue eyes unwavering, clear, and unyielding. "Apology accepted," he said. "It won't change everything, of course. Not now." He gestured toward the empty street, silent and watchful. "But it is a start. A small act of honesty in a world that seems to have forgotten what that word means."

We stood in silence for a long moment, the kind of silence that pressed down on you and yet gave room to breathe, to reflect, to feel the weight of what had been done and perhaps imagine the possibility of something better. He adjusted the telescope slightly; his hands were deliberate and calm. "The heavens are still speaking," he said softly. "If we are willing to listen."

I stepped back from the porch, my body lighter than when I had arrived, but not free. The guilt had not vanished; it still lingered, an echo in my chest and a whisper in my mind. But it had shifted. It was no longer a crushing weight of shame. It had become a reminder. A reminder of my fallibility, my need for grace, my tendency to judge too quickly. Admitting I was wrong hadn't solved the world's problems, hadn't fixed the silence, hadn't restored the neighborhood's trust in him. But it had cracked something within me, broken the hardened shell of pride and self-righteousness. And in that space, fragile and new, a tiny seed of humility took root. A seed that, perhaps, might grow, even in this quiet, uncertain world.

Imagine, for a moment, that the faults and burdens we carry in life are represented by a single stone. Each of us carries one. Smooth. Worn. Heavy. It is the stone of all our unadmitted faults, the lie we never corrected, the unkind word we never took back, the prideful refusal to say the words that rebuild and restore: *"I was wrong."*

This stone is a paradox. We polish it with self-justification, telling ourselves we were misunderstood, that the other person deserved it, that the fault was only partly ours. But every time we deny the truth, the stone does not shrink. It grows heavier. It drags our feet as we try to walk toward forgiveness. It blinds us when we try to look into the face of the one we have wronged.

Now imagine walking through a valley on a clear day. Above you, the sky is a flawless sapphire blue. Yet as you carry your stone, the air thickens—not with fog, but with the suffocating dust of self-deception. Soon, you can barely see the sun. You are isolated, not because God has abandoned you, but because your own resistance has created a storm of blinding darkness. You are in bondage to yourself.

Then comes relief. A quiet, trembling moment when you look at the stone and whisper, *"This is mine. I admit it. I am wrong."* And suddenly, that smooth, heavy rock feels lighter than a feather. Because this admission is not just to another person; it is an alignment of your small, defiant will with the vast, unyielding sovereignty of God. Admitting fault is not weakness; it is the ultimate act of spiritual strength. It is laying down your shield, choosing truth over pride.

Consider this: if we cannot humble ourselves to admit a simple fault to a neighbor, how can we stand ready before the Infinite Light? Scripture tells us that when the Lord calls us home, it will be in the twinkling of an eye. There will be no time for justifications, no time for excuses, no time to explain how it was complicated. We must already be unburdened and light. We must have practiced the posture of humility and selflessness.

Imagine that moment. A sound pierces the heavens, not a gentle chime, but a trumpet. In that instant, those still carrying their self-made stones are weighed down. Denial anchors them to the earth. Vision clouded by their personal dust storm, they cannot ascend. They are left in the rubble.

But those who have admitted their wrongs, whose hands are empty because they have laid down their stones, are free. Their bodies are no longer cages. Their souls have already ascended to truth. With nothing to hold them, nothing anchoring them to the weight of this world, they rise with the Lord. Their confession was preparation, a deliberate act of surrender, not born of terror, but of joyful expectation.

This is the Sound of Only. And when that time comes, will you be ready, or will you still be wondering?

Before we move forward, I ask you to sit with Isaiah's story, not as entertainment, not as inspiration, but as an explorer discovering the spiritual weight of unadmitted fault that each of us carries. Observe the profound freedom that comes from the simple, powerful act of saying, *"I was wrong."*

CHAPTER 7:
ASHES OF PRIDE

"Search me, God, and know my heart; test me and know my anxious thoughts. See if there is any offensive way in me, and lead me in the way everlasting."
- Psalms 139:23-24

Dr. Ruth Wilder had perfect hands; she had been told that her entire career. Steady, precise, capable of movements so minute they required magnification even to register, hands that had performed more than three thousand surgeries, hands that had saved lives, repaired failing hearts, given people years they were never meant to have, and hands that had taken something that had never been hers to take.

Ruth stood in her home office at four forty-seven a.m., the room illuminated only by the thin grey bleed of dawn through the tall windows, her gaze fixed on the filing cabinet in the corner. The power had been out for six hours. Long enough to be inconvenient and irritating. Nothing more than a municipal failure, a cascade of incompetence somewhere down the line, a systems issue she assumed would be corrected by people far less capable than she was. The stories she'd heard, the breathless reports from other cities, the religious hysteria about trumpets and vanished bodies and the end of everything, she dismissed with the same private disdain she reserved for bad research and emotional thinking. People believed nonsense because they needed meaning where there was only chaos.

The filing cabinet, however, mattered. Inside the bottom drawer were patient files, copies she had made over the years. Files she wasn't supposed to have, documentation that chronicled both her greatest professional achievements and her deepest professional sins, often within the same manila folder. Ruth Wilder was fifty-three years old. Chief of Cardiology at Illinois Masonic Hospital. Published in every major medical journal that mattered. Sought after for consultations across the country. A reputation built on excellence, innovation, and results that other surgeons simply could not replicate.

Her office reflected that reputation. Dark wood shelving lined the walls, heavy with textbooks and bound journals. Awards were framed, not ostentatiously, but deliberately, positioned at eye level where they belonged. A mahogany desk dominated the center of the room, immaculate, authoritative, chosen less for comfort than for presence. Everything in the space spoke of order, discipline, and earned superiority.

And yet, hidden in a locked drawer of that filing cabinet was the truth.

She cut corners. Not with patient care. Never with the surgeries themselves, her technical skill was beyond reproach. But with protocol. With documentation. With the bureaucratic machinery that governed modern medicine, and, in Ruth's opinion, frequently obstructed the act of actually saving lives. She performed procedures without proper authorization when she knew they were necessary. Altered records to make treatments appear more conventional than they were. Introduced techniques lifted from experimental protocols without waiting for approval. Prescribed medications off-label without the mandated consultations.

And she documented everything not out of guilt or fear but because Ruth was a scientist. She documented deviations, unauthorized procedures, calculated risks that paid off, and the rare ones that didn't. Data mattered. Outcomes mattered. Permission was secondary.

The files were her private research, her real work, the version she was actually proud of, stripped of the sanitized language she presented to ethics boards and hospital administrators, free from the careful phrasing that made risk sound reasonable and deviation sound approved. There was also evidence, evidence that could dismantle her career, her reputation, the legacy she had spent decades building, evidence that documented dozens of violations, even if the outcomes had been good, even if patients were still alive because she had been willing to do what others would not. Ruth had always told herself the files were safe, that no one knew they existed, that her home office was private territory protected by distance and discretion, and the simple belief that institutions did not reach into people's homes unless invited.

That belief had held until her phone died. Not slipped into silence the way outages sometimes did, not drained slowly, but gone entirely, hours earlier, leaving her cut off in a way that felt suddenly deliberate, and when the hospital still hadn't called, she told herself it was logistics, that they were managing, that administrators were scrambling as they always did when systems failed. It was only later, when a runner arrived, an actual person sent on foot to inform department heads that the hospital was operating in crisis mode, emergency power only, all elective procedures cancelled, that something in her chest tightened.

And then came the audit, A mandatory review of all patient records and physician files scheduled to begin as soon as the systems were restored, random in selection, comprehensive in scope, the kind of process that did not care about brilliance or intention or outcomes, only compliance. The words settled slowly, sinking past her confidence, past the arguments she had rehearsed for years about necessity and innovation, until they reached the place she had kept carefully sealed. An audit did not weigh lives saved against rules broken. It counted infractions. And Ruth had built her reputation by stepping over them.

She turned back to the filing cabinet, and for the first time, it no longer felt like storage. It felt like a witness, an accusation, a record of every compromise she had justified in the name of results, pulsing faintly in the dim light as the distance between her public brilliance and her private truth began to collapse.

Random meant everything. Home offices. Personal files. Anything that might contain patient information or documentation of care. In normal times, Ruth would have had weeks of warning, time to sanitize, time to make certain documents disappear, time to rehearse her explanations and refine her justifications. But these were not normal times. The power was out. The phones were dead. The internet was gone. And if the stories were true, if the trumpet had already sounded or was about to, then time itself was no longer something she could assume she had.

Ruth crossed the room to the filing cabinet, pulled the key from her desk drawer, unlocked the bottom drawer, and opened it. Forty-three files. Forty-three patients whose care had involved some deviation from standard protocol, some minor, some substantial, all documented in her precise handwriting and accompanied by outcome data that showed, in most cases, excellent results.

Ruth pulled out the first file. Naomi Gilmore. Seventy-six. Severe aortic stenosis. The standard approach would have been valve replacement, the safe answer, the approved one, but Ruth had refined a repair technique that was still classified as experimental, stalled in committees that barely understood it. It had worked. Naomi had walked out of the hospital two weeks later and, as far as Ruth knew, was still alive five years on. The procedure hadn't been approved. Ruth had made the call in the operating room, in the moment, based on what she saw when she opened Naomi's chest, trusting her own assessment over a protocol written by people who would never hold a beating heart in their hands. She hadn't waited for permission because she hadn't needed it. She had been right.

How was that wrong?

Her hands trembled slightly as she held the file. Her perfect hands. Her surgeon's hands. Shaking. She set Naomi's file on the desk and pulled out another. David Garcia. Fifty-one. Complex coronary artery disease. Ruth had used a drug combination that wasn't approved for his specific presentation, a combination trapped in endless review cycles, discussed and rediscussed by people who valued caution over action. It had prevented a second heart attack. David had lived another three years before dying peacefully in his sleep from unrelated causes. Another deviation. Another calculated decision. Another life was extended because she had refused to wait.

File after file. Patient after patient. A career's worth of moments where Ruth had looked at the rules and dismissed them, where she had weighed the abstract risk of breaking protocol against the very real consequences of following it and chosen her own judgment every time. She had never doubted those decisions. The outcomes had proven her right. Saving lives mattered more than paperwork, more than committees, more than approval processes designed to protect institutions from liability rather than patients from death.

She had known she was right, and that knowledge had been enough.

But now, looking at the files spread across her desk in the grainy pre-dawn light, Ruth was no longer sure. Not because the outcomes were bad. The outcomes were excellent. That was what made this unbearable. She had **broken** the brokenthe rules, and people had lived. She had violated protocols, and hearts had been repaired. She had ignored guidelines, and patients had walked out of her hospital when other surgeons would have stopped, would have followed procedure, would have accepted loss as policy.

And yet, she had also played God. That was the truth she had avoided for twenty years, buried beneath outcomes and data and justification. Every decision to override protocol, every moment she chose her judgment over established procedure, carried the same unspoken declaration. I know better. I am smarter than the system. I am more capable than the committees, ethics boards, and regulatory bodies that move slowly while people die. Trust me instead of trusting the rules. She had made herself the authority. The final arbiter. Her own god.

Ruth lowered herself into her chair, surrounded by the evidence of her professional life, the good and the bad so tightly intertwined they could no longer be separated, excellence and arrogance housed in the same Manila folders, lives are saved through methods that could destroy her if exposed. Fear pressed in now, not sudden or panicked, but heavy and deliberate, settling into her chest as inevitability rather than possibility. The audit was coming. Maybe not today. Maybe not this week. But if the power returned, if systems rebooted, if society rebuilt itself into something recognizable again, the audit would happen. And these files would be found.

Unless she destroyed them, the thought turned her stomach. These files were her real work. Her actual achievements. The moments she had been brave enough to trust herself, skilled enough to succeed, bold enough to push past rules written by people who never stepped into an operating theatre. Destroying them felt like erasing herself, like reducing her career to the sanitized, approved, bureaucratically acceptable version that had never mattered to her in the first place.

But keeping them meant preserving evidence of her pride. Proof of her refusal to submit to any authority higher than her own judgment.

Anger flared beneath the fear then, sharp and resentful. At a system that punished innovation. At processes designed to protect institutions rather than patients. At committees that would dissect her decisions from behind conference tables, never acknowledging that their caution had cost lives, too.

Ruth reached into her desk and pulled out the lighter. She didn't smoke, never had, but she kept it for candles during outages. Now it sat beside the files, small and silver, absurdly simple, capable of reducing twenty years of work to ash.

Ruth flipped open the lighter. The small flame danced in the dim room. She nudged Naomi's file over the metal wastebasket, one of the few she still kept, because she appreciated things that lasted. Her hand hovered. What was she destroying? The evidence of her crime or the record of her competence? The answer was obvious. Both. They were inseparable. She couldn't erase the protocol violations without erasing the lives she had saved, couldn't cleanse the record of her arrogance without erasing her achievements.

The flame licked her palm, hot and insistent. Ruth held it steady, watching its tiny dance, thinking about the stories she'd heard: the trumpet, people vanishing, clothes left behind in cars, in hospital beds, patients gone the next moment. If any of it was true, the audit was meaningless. Survival, judgment, those were the real questions.

And these files, these meticulous records of her professional pride, were evidence. Not just of protocol violations, but of a deeper condition, one she had cultivated in herself over decades: the conviction that she was the final authority, that her judgment outweighed every rule, every committee, every board. She had played God on every chest she opened, repairing hearts and bending systems to her will. Now, it felt as if something was opening her own chest, exposing her heart, revealing the truth she had long ignored.

Massive pride had driven her to excellence, but it had also isolated her, convinced her that she knew better than everyone else, that she was the center of her own universe. The lighter heated her palm, and she set it down, unwilling to burn just yet. She looked again at the files: forty-three of them, forty-three witnesses to her competence and her arrogance, forty-three records of a brilliant surgeon who had saved lives and a proud woman who refused to submit to anything or anyone. Both were true. Both existed in the same person, in the same career, in the same files.

And now she had to decide. Keep the files and risk exposure if the audit came, preserve the evidence of her skill alongside the evidence of her pride, complete and damning in equal measure, or destroy them, erase everything, leave only the sanitized version, safe but empty. Destroy the bad, but also destroy the good, because the two could never be separated.

Ruth stood and walked to the window, the flame still flickering in her mind, and for the first time, the certainty she had always carried felt heavier than it had ever been.

The street outside was empty. Silent. The sun was just beginning to rise, painting the sky in shades of pink and gold that felt almost obscene against the quiet and the uncertainty, against the strange weight pressing in on Ruth's chest. She didn't know for certain what had happened. The power was out. Communication was dead. Phones, internet, networks, all gone. But that didn't mean the rapture had occurred. It could be a cascade of failures, an infrastructure breakdown, something explainable and mundane. She wanted to believe that, wanted to believe the world could return to normal, and she'd have time to deal with the files properly, systematically, on her own schedule.

But deep in her chest, in the place where instinct and experience combined to produce certainty in the operating room, Ruth knew. Something had happened. Something final. Something that changed everything. And standing at the window, watching the sunrise over an empty street, she understood what she needed to do. Not for the audit, not for fear of consequences. But for something she had ignored for twenty years while perfecting her techniques, building her reputation, documenting every deviation from protocol. Something unquantifiable, unmeasurable, dismissed for its irrelevance to medicine, the soul. The part of a person no surgery could touch, the part that judgment would reach.

Ruth walked back to her desk and picked up the lighter again. This time, she lit Naomi Gilmore's file. The paper caught instantly. She dropped it into the metal wastebasket, flames consuming notes, outcome data, and records of lives saved through unauthorized means. It hurt, physically hurt, like watching a piece of herself burn. She reached for the next file, David Garcia lit it, dropped it, watched it flare. File after file, patient after patient, her evidence, her career, her audacity reduced to ash.

She did not cry. Years in operating rooms had taught her to control her emotions, to make the hard decisions without sentiment, to do what needed to be done regardless of how it felt. This was no different. Whether judgment was coming, whether the world was ending, this had to be done. She could not stand before God, or the idea of God, and defend these files. Could not say, yes, I violated protocols, yes, I made myself the final authority, yes, I played God with people's lives, but look at the outcomes. Look at how many survived. Because outcomes didn't matter. Submission did. Acknowledging authority beyond herself mattered. And the evidence in these forty-three files said she had refused. She had lived as her own god.

And yet, as the last file burned, she felt lighter. Strange, unexpected. The weight of carrying two selves, the sanitized public Ruth and the real Ruth, had lifted. The exhaustion of trusting only herself, of being the sole authority in every decision, was gone. Her pride, her arrogance, her insistence on perfection, burned away with the paper.

And in that moment, almost imperceptibly, a small spark flickered in her chest. A thought she would have laughed at hours ago. Maybe, just maybe, this was the rapture. The outages, the silence, the empty streets, they were not meaningless. Maybe this was the end. Maybe burning the files had been a way to hide from God, a futile attempt to protect herself from judgment, and yet… the act of destruction, the letting go, had left her lighter, cleaner, and for the first time, open to the possibility that she was not the only authority, that maybe there was something higher, something final, watching, and that her defiance had been both brilliant and irrelevant, and that in the end, she could no longer pretend she alone determined the measure of right and wrong.

She sat back, breathing smoke and ash, staring at the empty filing cabinet drawer, open, bare, ready to be filled, or to remain empty. Either way, the old records were gone. And for the first time in decades, Ruth Wilder felt as though she could breathe, as though some small piece of her arrogance had finally been humbled, just enough to wonder if the stories she had dismissed might be real.

Ruth sat back in her chair, the metal wastebasket smoldering faintly at her side, ash curling like smoke tendrils into the dim light of her office. She leaned forward, elbows resting on the desk, and for the first time really looked at herself in the reflection of the small dancing flames, the firelight catching the angles of her face, the sharp line of her jaw, the intensity in her eyes, the confidence that had carried her through decades of impossible decisions. There she was, in the flicker, a woman who had bent systems to her will, who had trusted herself when everyone else hesitated, who had chosen her judgment over every committee, every guideline, every so-called authority, and the reflection did not betray doubt or weakness. It only amplified her.

She smiled faintly, a curve of lips that knew it had always been right. "Stupid," she murmured, almost amused at the thought. "All of it. The stories, the whispers, the trumpet, the vanished people, the rapture, absurd, and had nothing to do with her. "I've done everything anyone could do, better than anyone else. And no god is watchingthere is no god watching, no judgment, no cosmic accounting. Nothing except me. And I've survived every second of it."

The flame wavered, and she caught its reflection again, saw herself in it, strong, capable, untouchable. "Prove me wrong," she said aloud, her voice quiet but sharp, deliberate, echoing softly in the stillness of the office. "If you're out there, prove me wrong." She leaned back, considered the wastebasket, and with the precision of a surgeon, poured a small pitcher of water over the smoldering flames. The fire hissed, spat, and died, leaving only smoke and ash curling toward the ceiling.

Ruth woke from her nap to the pale light of late morning filtering through the blinds, the quiet hum of the world outside barely reaching her. She sat upright in bed, stretching slowly. **She** reached for her robe, a silk blend in muted cream, weighty in its drape, perfectly tailored, the kind of understated luxury that announced competence rather than wealth, and tied it at her waist with calm authority, the smooth belt sliding through her fingers as if it, too, understood precision. She rose from the bed steadily, barefoot on the hardwood, each step deliberate, controlled, aware of the world but above its urgency.

The power was still out, but it mattered little. Making coffee by hand suited her perfectly. She enjoyed the methodical rhythm, the grind of beans, the measured pour of water, the small, tactile satisfaction of control, of knowing that nothing she touched could fail, even the simplest ritual. Her hands, which had repaired hearts, which had defied protocol with perfect precision, moved now with the same confidence she always carried.

A sudden banging on the door cut through the quiet. Ruth paused, a little annoyed. She moved toward the door with slow, controlled steps, swaying slightly in the silk of her robe, entirely in command of herself, entirely unconcerned with alarm or urgency.

Darrion stood there, shoulders hunched, chest rising and falling rapidly, ginger hair plastered to his pale forehead, sweat gleaming along his temples. Even standing still, he radiated urgency. He had always understood, always known enough about her deviations to keep her secrets without speaking them aloud. Ruth regarded him coolly, letting her gaze sweep over the flushed, disheveled nurse.

"Darrion," she said, voice sharp but measured, carrying the authority she had honed over decades, "You're here at my house. Explain yourself. What's wrong?"

He raised a hand to his chest, trying to catch his breath, and finally gasped out, "The peds patient... the one with the complex congenital hypertrophic cardiomyopathy, post-op... she just... passed away. Her vitals were stable, post-op everything was fine, and then, thirty minutes ago, she flatlined."

The air seemed to shift. Ruth's eyes narrowed, her grip on the doorframe tightening without breaking her composure entirely. Sweat prickled at her temples. "What? Explain. Her ejection fraction? LVOT? Coronary flow? Arrhythmias? What went wrong?"

Darrion's voice was steady but urgent, his exhaustion visible. "Everything was normal, Ruth. Labs, echo, pressures, perfect. Except... you tried the modified repair, the minor experimental adjustment you never cleared with the board. Not risky, not major, just... unapproved."

Ruth's chest rose and fell quickly. Her vision narrowed. Her mind raced over the surgery, the measurements, the modifications she had made with careful calculation. "But she tolerated it perfectly. This was an easy case. Everything was correct. The pressures, the flow... nothing was abnormal. This is impossible. How?"

Darrion shook his head slowly. "I don't know. And the parents are they're threatening a lawsuit. Legal is asking for the files. We can't find them. Do you have them?"

Ruth stood silent for a moment, hands gripping the doorframe, eyes staring past him, unfocused. Slowly, she shook her head. Nothing. Silence.

Darrion turned to leave, shoulders heavy, then paused. He met her gaze over his shoulder. "I knew the risks you always took, thinking you were God. But you're not. There's a God above us all. You save lives, yes, but can you save yourself from this?"

And then he was gone, leaving Ruth alone, leaning against the frame, chest heaving.

Ruth slammed the door behind her and ran. Her robe swirled around her legs as she rushed past the kitchen to the drawing room. She fell to the floor in front of the heap of ash where the files had burned. Her hands plunged into the cold, crumbling remains, fingers scraping through what had been her life's work.

Angel. She remembered the child's name. The pediatric patient. The little girl whose parents had told her why they named her so. And now she was gone. Ruth's hands shook, her chest heaving. The arrogance that had carried her for decades drained away, leaving only raw panic.

Ruth fell to her knees in front of the heap of ash, hands clawing through it as if she could dig back the life she had destroyed. Her chest heaved violently, each sob tearing from her throat like it had its own life. She gasped, shuddered, let out ragged, uneven wails that rattled through her ribcage. Tears ran unchecked, hot and stinging, smearing the gray ash across her cheeks and into her hair. Her nose ran, her lips trembled, her jaw locked and unclenched in uneven bursts.

She cried with a sound that was raw and animal, guttural, a sound of disbelief and regret and uncontained sorrow. Her fingers dug into the ash, pressing and tearing, as if punishing herself could bring the child back. Her back arched, head thrown forward, and she let the weight of all the arrogance she had carried for decades crumble out of her. There was no composure, no pride, no rationalizing, just the unbearable, ugly pain of knowing she had overstepped, that she had failed in a way no skill or brilliance could undo.

Every heartbeat felt sharp in her chest, every breath came ragged and uneven. Her sobs shook her shoulders, her arms, her entire body, and still she cried, because the child's name, Angel, and the image of her small, trusting face would not leave her. She cried until the sound was raw in her throat, until her body was trembling and trembling and trembling again, and the arrogance that had once defined her felt like a distant, meaningless memory, leaving only grief, regret, and the hollow ache of failure.

The sobs didn't stop. They rattled her chest, wracked her shoulders, trembled through her fingers as they clawed through the ash. And then, between one ragged breath and the next, something settled in her mind, a truth she had been too arrogant to see. The audit, the warnings, the whispers, the power outage, the chaos, it wasn't random. It wasn't meaningless. It was a chance, a warning, a hand extended, a hit to make her stop before she truly broke. And she had ignored it. She had dismissed it, laughed at it, believed herself above it. She had played God. And now, the consequences had landed squarely in her lap.

She pressed her hands to her face, chest heaving, and whispered through gasps and tears, "God… if you're there… if you're really there… I…I've been… I've been stupid, I've been arrogant, I've been… I've been doing beendoing everything wrong. I thought I knew better, I thought I could control everything, that my hands, my brain, my judgment… that they were enough. But I… I can't fix this. I can't. I don't… I don't know how to make this right. I, I failed her, God… Angel… I failed her. I failed. I failed. Please… I don't know… I don't know what to do."

Her voice cracked, raw and ragged. She cried louder, a sound full of despair, full of confusion, full of self-loathing. "I… I thought I could be God! I thought I could decide who lives and who dies! I thought I could bend rules and everything would be okay… and it's not okay. It's never okay. I… I can't… I can't do this alone. I can't… I can't fix her, I can't fix them, I can't… I can't save myself. I'm sorry. I am so sorry!"

She paused only to inhale raggedly, tears spilling freely, makeup streaked, hair clinging to her wet cheeks. She buried her face in her hands again, rocking slightly on the floor, letting it all out— arrogance, pride, guilt, helplessness. And then, through the tears and trembling, she lifted her head.

Her reflection in the glass of the drawing room window caught her, fractured by the morning light. Once, she would have seen a precise, flawless version of herself: hair perfect, posture impeccable, hands steady, every line measured, every edge sharp. That was Ruth, polished, controlled, untouchable, the image she had presented to the world for decades.

Now… she saw herself. Hair loose, damp, and matted to her face, robe askew, shoulders trembling, hands smudged with ash, eyes red and swollen from crying. This was her. Not the polished version. Not the version she had controlled with arrogance and precision. The one in the reflection was broken, messy, raw, and real. And for the first time, she let herself accept it.

She whispered through trembling lips, almost to herself, almost to God, "I… I can't do this alone. I can't fix it. I can't fix her. I can't… I can't control anything anymore. Please… help me. Teach me. Show me how not to be… not to be God. I give it to you. I don't want to be God. I… I'm yours. I…I'm yours."

She let her forehead rest on the floor, hands splayed in the ash, body shaking, finally surrendering.

She let her forehead rest on the floor, hands splayed in the ash, body shaking, sobs rattling through her chest, every bit of control she had built over decades gone. She was raw. She was undone. She was completely human. And yet, through the ragged breaths and tears, through the ache and the guilt that seemed too heavy to bear, clarity began to edge its way in.

She knew exactly what she needed to do. She needed to confess her sins. She needed to face the consequences of her mistakes. She needed to pay for the arrogance that had made her play God, the experiments she had justified to herself, the lives she had touched with her own reckless certainty. She needed to be accountable, fully and utterly, with no excuses left in her arsenal, no pride to shield her.

And maybe just maybe if she could do that, if she could own everything, if she could bear it all and give it over fully, she could begin to forgive herself. And maybe... maybe then, God would forgive her too.

She remained on the floor, eyes fixed on the gray ash, chest rising and falling with the rhythm of grief and clarity entwined, the reflection in the glass no longer a polished mask but the undeniable truth of who she was. Broken. Human. Guilty. And finally, ready to do what was necessary.

If there's one thing I hope you take from Ruth's story, it's this: being smart, being skilled, being confident, none of that makes you untouchable. Ruth thought she could control everything, bend the rules, play God, and get away with it because she believed she was better than everyone else. And for a while, it worked; people lived, hearts were saved, and she felt untouchable. But in the end, life has a way of catching up. What she couldn't control, what she ignored, slammed into her, and she had to face the truth: pride and arrogance can blind you, and no skill can replace accountability. The lesson isn't that she failed as a surgeon, it's that she forgot to be human. And the real strength, the part that really matters, comes from owning your mistakes, feeling the weight of them, and trying to make them right.

CHAPTER 8:
HOLLOW PRAYERS

"He who covers his sins will not prosper, but whoever confesses and forsakes them will obtain mercy."
- **Proverbs 28:13**

Benjamin returned home, the evening sky outside dim and strange without the familiar glow of streetlights. He had walked the neighborhood, scanning for signs of life, neighbors on porches, cars idling in driveways, but all houses were dark, silent, and no sign of life. The air carried the faint smell of rain on hot asphalt, and somewhere down the street, a dog barked once, then nothing.

Inside, Esther was standing near the counter, her brow furrowed under the soft candlelight they'd lit to compensate for the blackout. "Ben, what's wrong?" she asked, her voice calm but edged with unease.

"I don't know," he said, shrugging as he set down his keys. "It's just a power outage. Probably nothing. Don't worry."

Esther's eyes searched his face, but she didn't press. Instead, she lowered her voice, leaning closer. "People are saying... It's the rapture."

Benjamin chuckled lightly, brushing it off. "Well, that's good, isn't it?" He moved toward the table, a practiced smile on his face. "We always pray, we always ask for forgiveness. Everything's fine."

The candlelight flickered across their small living room. The table was modestly set: a steaming pot of simple stew, bread from the bakery around the corner, and glasses of water. His children, Sara and Joshua, sat opposite him, their clothes rumpled from a long day, faces glowing faintly in the golden light. Sara twirled a strand of hair around her finger, frowning at the shadows; Joshua picked at the bread.

Benjamin pulled out the chairs and sat down, lifting his hands and his family's hands in place. He glanced at Esther, then at his children, feeling the familiar satisfaction of being the head of the household, the man guiding prayer, the Christian leading his family.

"Let's pray," he said, voice steady and confident.

He closed his eyes. "Dear Lord," he began, the words flowing smoothly, like a well-rehearsed speech, "Thank You for this food, for keeping our family safe, for giving us another day. Please bless this meal."

He squeezed their hands. "Amen."

The words hung in the air; they felt proper and polished, but inside him, there was no tremor of fear, no sense of awe or real weight of confession, just simple words. Rituals he had learned, repeated often enough to convince himself that God saw him as upright, righteous. Benjamin glanced at his wife, her hair catching the candlelight, soft expression, hands folded over his, and at his children, and nodded internally, they were fine, everything was fine.

Dinner began. Spoonfuls of stew, bread torn and shared, occasional small chatter about school, homework, plans for tomorrow. Benjamin's mind wandered just enough to notice Esther smiling at a joke Joshua made, Sara rolling her eyes at her brother, the warmth in their small living room flickering in rhythm with the candles.

He believed he was a good Christian. Sure, he made mistakes, but they were small. Minor. Easily forgivable. A temper here, a lie there, a glance where it shouldn't be, but nothing catastrophic. He was doing everything that mattered: praying, giving thanks, confessing in the right places, leading his family properly; that was enough.

The faith felt effortless and a little careless, but that's how he liked it. It didn't demand that he look too closely, that he examine his heart. It didn't make him stop and think about the anger he hadn't really controlled, the lies he hadn't truly repented of, the pride he defended with every word. It was neat, contained, like the stew in front of him: warm, filling, enough to survive, enough to feel comforted, but not enough to challenge him.

The house was quiet after dinner. The children had gone to bed, yawns still clinging to their faces, and Esther had tidied the table before retreating upstairs. Benjamin lingered in the drawing room, the familiar space dim in the flickering candlelight. The blackout had left the room strangely still, the shadows deepening the corners, making the furniture feel heavier, older. The couch he slumped into sagged slightly under his weight, a worn, overstuffed thing with fabric softened from years of use. The rug beneath his feet was patterned and threadbare at the edges, the coffee table cluttered with remotes, coasters, and yesterday's newspaper. Behind the chair, tucked in the small space where it wouldn't be noticed, was a stack of magazines, dog-eared, marked, and well-used.

Benjamin reached for one without a second thought, sliding it from its hiding spot. He flipped through the pages casually, barely glancing at the images, feeling no guilt whatsoever. A good Christian, he told himself that constantly. This was a minor indulgence, a basic human need. Everyone did it, he reasoned, as it was nothing major or harmful, healthy even.

A soft creak sounded from the doorway. "Ben… why aren't you in bed?" Esther's voice was gentle, tinged with sleepiness. She stood there clad in a simple, long-sleeved nightdress, the fabric loose and plain, nothing meant to seduce, only enough to be modest and comfortable.

Benjamin jolted upright, hastily trying to hide the magazine behind him. He caught her eyes, immediately seeing the hurt flicker there. His chest tightened not with shame, but irritation.

"Just go to bed," he said sharply, voice brittle. "I'll be there soon."

Esther hesitated, her gaze soft but persistent. He let himself feel a flare of annoyance. "Go away, Esther. Give a man some peace, for God's sake," he said, louder this time, his tone thick with irritation and self-righteousness.

From the shadows behind her, small figures appeared, Sara and Joshua, blinking sleep from their eyes, drawn by the raised voice. Benjamin's irritation deepened. He felt cornered, judged. Their presence wasn't comforting; it was an intrusion. His peace, his small sanctuary, was being disrupted.

"Take them with you," he snapped, his pride inflating with every word. *I love my kids,* he told himself, *but every man needs his time. I work so hard to keep the house going; I deserve a little time to myself.*

Esther's lips pressed into a thin line. Her hands gently held the children close, and her long nightdress brushed the floor as she turned and walked toward the stairs, the kids clinging to the soft fabric at the hem, their tiny hands seeking reassurance. Benjamin watched them go, satisfied that they'd obeyed, yet strangely untouched by remorse.

He leaned back into the couch, the worn fabric welcoming him, and retrieved the magazine he had tried to hide. The pages were familiar and comforting, a quiet indulgence that required no compromise. The anger ebbed, replaced by a smug sense of entitlement. No one understood a man's need for quiet time, for a moment to himself, not his wife or his children.

Minutes passed, and the candlelight flickered, and shadows stretched. Benjamin continued flipping through the pages, letting the images wash over him. Slowly, the weight of the day, the tension of the exchange and the comfort of his secret indulgence lulled him into drowsiness. He slouched deeper into the couch, eyes closing.

Benjamin's chest rose and fell in easy rhythm, the magazine resting loosely in his lap. He slept there, unconcerned, uncaring, his mind not troubled by her hurt or the disapproval that lingered like a faint shadow in the room. His world was simple. His peace was earned, he thought.

The next morning, Benjamin woke late, the sunlight faint through the drawn curtains, streaking across the floorboards of the drawing room. His back ached from sleeping on the couch, the stiffness making every movement sluggish and heavy. He stretched with a groan, rubbing at his shoulders, eyes squinting as the dull morning light hit him.

Yawning, he pushed himself up and shuffled toward the bedroom, expecting to find Esther tucked under the blankets. His steps were slow, sleepy, heavy, dragging across the carpet, the ache in his back a constant reminder of his slouched posture on the couch. But when he reached the room, it was empty. No rustling sheets, no small bodies nestled under the covers.

He blinked, confused. "Esther?" His voice was soft, hoarse from sleep. The quiet answered him. The room smelled faintly of lavender from her night oil, but the bed was empty. His sleepy haze began to fade, replaced with a flicker of unease.

He padded toward the bathroom, still rubbing at his sore back, expecting perhaps to find her there. Nothing. The mirror reflected only his own worried, tired face. "Maybe… she fell asleep with the kids," he muttered, more to calm himself than out of certainty. Esther didn't like sleeping alone on nights like this; when he stayed up late or came home after long nights, she often brought the children into the master bed.

But now, the bed was empty. And when he checked the children's rooms, neither Sara nor Joshua was there either.

The flicker of concern ignited into real worry, spreading tight and hot in his chest. "Esther! Sara! Joshua!" he called, louder this time, pacing down the hallway. The sound of his own voice bouncing off the walls was unnerving. He strained to hear Sara's soft giggle, Joshua's tentative steps, Esther's low humming that always eased the house, but the silence returned, oppressive and thick.

He rushed from room to room, throwing open doors, heart hammering, every corner and closet checked. Panic edged into his voice as he yelled their names again, each call sharper, more desperate. "Esther! Kids! Where are you?"

Nothing.

The chill of the morning seeped through the walls, but he didn't stop. Without a robe, without shoes, he burst out into the yard, the cold biting at his bare feet, the grass damp and slick beneath him. He ran up the street, peering into windows, scanning every yard, every corner of the block, calling their names, fear gnawing at him, twisting his chest. But the neighborhood was still, eerily silent under the dim morning light.

Returning home, he felt the helplessness crush him. He stumbled through the front door, sliding to the lounge floor as if his legs had no strength of their own. His knees hit the carpet, rough and grounding, but it didn't comfort him. His breath came in ragged bursts, and for a moment, he just collapsed, forehead pressed against the floor, unable to speak. *Where are they? Why aren't they here? What's happening?*

He tried to call out again, but his throat tightened with panic, the power outage muting the world around him, the silence pressing down like a weight. Tears burned his eyes, running unchecked, his hands shaking as they pressed into the floor beneath him. The lounge, once a place of quiet indulgence, now felt hollow, confining, a cage.

And there, on the ground, Benjamin finally let himself surrender to the panic that had been building, the frantic search, the impossible emptiness around him. He wept, not caring who might hear, not thinking of anything beyond the absence of his wife and children, the sudden, terrifying reality that they were gone, somewhere he could not reach.

Benjamin staggered from room to room, the emptiness of the house swallowing him whole, pressing in on all sides, the silence unbearable. First, he stumbled into the drawing room, the same room where he had slumped over the couch just last night, a magazine in hand, indulging in something he told himself was harmless, normal, and human. The memory hit him like a blow: the magazine spread open, the quiet selfishness, the irritation when Esther had interrupted him, the anger, the sense of entitlement. It wasn't just the act, it was the casual disregard, the arrogance, the belief that it was all permissible because he was a good Christian. *This was my sin*, he thought, the taste of guilt sour in his mouth for the first time.

He moved on, feet dragging, into the children's bedroom. Joshua's small violin rested in its corner, its strings slightly out of tune, and the memory that rose made his stomach twist. How he had once snapped it in two because he thought it was a "girly" instrument, convinced he was teaching his son strength, discipline, righteousness, even, doing it all *for his own good*. He had thought himself a protector, a teacher of toughness, but now the memory felt like a wound, raw and self-serving, the arrogance of thinking he knew better than his child.

The hallway felt longer than it was, his steps unsteady as he entered his bedroom. The memory of last night wasn't enough; the one from months ago came flooding in, how he had yelled at Esther for wearing the simple, modest nightdress she always chose, for never bothering with fancy clothes, for not being like other wives, for not dressing *sexy* just because he desired it. How he had demanded more from her while praising himself as the wise, fair husband, convinced that he knew what was best for the family. The shame burned hotter now, raw and undeniable.

And then he returned to the lounge, the heart of the house, the place where so much of his pride and neglect had quietly festered. Sara's face, tear-streaked from a bullying incident at school, came unbidden to him. He had been late to go out with friends, leaving Esther to handle the heartbreak, assuming she could, assuming she should, never considering that she needed him just as much as the kids did. He had taken pride in his efficiency, in his logic, in his careful calculations of what was "best for everyone," but now, walking alone through the hollow house, he saw it for what it was: selfishness disguised as righteousness, thoughtlessness disguised as wisdom.

Back in the lounge, he sank to his knees, the emptiness of the house pressing down like a weight he could not lift. The warmth, the laughter, the love of his family all gone, all suddenly absent, and with it came the full realization of the extent of his sins. They weren't small, trivial, or forgivable anymore; they were the accumulation of years of arrogance, of thinking himself always right, of thinking himself good while causing quiet hurt in every corner of this house.

The tears came then, uncontrolled, streaming down his face as he pressed his forehead into the floor, shaking, broken. The shame, the guilt, the grief merged into a single, suffocating wave. He could feel the entirety of his carelessness, selfishness, and moral blindness settle on him, a weight too heavy for one man to bear. And in that moment, on the cold floor, alone, Benjamin finally understood: he had been wrong in every quiet, subtle way, and now, in the absence of his family, he faced the full, devastating consequences of his soul.

Benjamin was a middle manager at a local insurance firm, a position he had clawed his way to over decades of long hours and meticulous work. He had always been proud of it, proud of the stability it provided his family, proud of the respect it earned him in his community. He attended the First Baptist Church every Sunday without fail, always sitting near the front, making sure the pastor noticed his devotion, and sometimes volunteering for small duties to reinforce the image of a good, upright Christian. He went to church regularly, prayed without fail, and insisted that these acts of faith outweighed the little human failings he indulged in, the impatience, the pride, the moments of selfishness. To him, they were not sins but small shortcomings, little blemishes that made him human, harmless imperfections that God would surely understand. He had convinced himself that his devotion, his prayers, and his hard work balanced the ledger of his life, and that in the grand scheme, he was a good man, one whose errors were minor and excusable, a man striving as best he could in a world that demanded compromise.

Benjamin sat on the cold floor of his lounge, the empty house pressing in on him. Dawn light seeped through the blinds, illuminating the photographs on the wall: vacations, birthdays, Christmas mornings, moments now gone while he remained. God, please remove my shortcomings. The prayer felt hollow. Meaningless. Seven years he had whispered it, and nothing had changed. Not because God had refused, but because he had never truly let go. He had asked for a transformation while clutching everything he was supposed to release. He had defended his sins, excused his anger, pride, lies, and lust, and convinced himself that his prayers made him righteous despite his choices. He wanted the appearance of holiness without its cost, and now, in the silence, the illusion collapsed.

Benjamin rose and looked at his reflection in front of the mirror, staring at the man he had defended for so long. Older, harder, familiar yet unrecognizable. "I've been lying," he whispered, voice cracking. "For seven years, I asked You to remove my shortcomings, but I didn't mean it. I wanted credit for wanting change, without ever actually changing." He pressed his palms against the sink, the cold marble grounding him. "I kept my anger because it made me feel powerful. I kept my pride because admitting I was wrong was humiliating. I kept everything and asked you to take it away." Tears came unbidden. For the first time, he felt the weight of his choices without excuses.

Benjamin fell to his knees. Not the polished prayers he recited at church, not the neat formulas he had repeated for years, but something raw, unprotected. "I surrender," he whispered. "All of it. The anger. The lies. The pride. The lust. The envy. The blame-shifting. I release them. I confess them. I repent of defending them instead of letting them go." He realized that his sins were not minor failings or understandable human shortcomings; they were choices he had repeated, defended, and nurtured. And now, the defenses were gone. God had not removed his sins; He had removed

Benjamin's ability to excuse them was the beginning of a real transformation.

He stood, stripped his Sunday suit, tie, and polished shoes, symbols of the image he had performed for years, and burned them in the backyard fire pit. The costume of holiness went up in flames. Back inside, he changed into plain clothes, showered, and knelt in the living room where his family had gathered. "God, I can't change myself," he prayed. "I've been asking for freedom while defending what I shouldn't. I'm defenseless now. I'm weak. Change me. Transform me. Not for appearances, not to feel better, but for real. I choose to let go. I choose to surrender. Help me cooperate with Your strength, because I cannot do this alone."

For the first time, Benjamin felt clarity piercing the hollow patterns of his life. The excuses were gone, the justifications removed, the defenses stripped away. All that remained was truth and the possibility of change. Not easy. Not guaranteed. But real. And in that truth, kneeling on the floor of his empty house, he finally understood the cost of real surrender, and the chance he had been denying himself for seven long years.

We like to pretend that small sins don't matter, that keeping a little anger, a little pride, a little lust tucked away is harmless, that we can pray while holding onto the very things we claim we want freedom from. Benjamin's story rips that lie apart. It's ugly. It's brutal. You can work hard, go to church, recite prayers, feed your image of goodness, and still rot inside. You can ask God to remove your shortcomings while feeding them, defending them, justifying them, and convince yourself you're a good person, but the truth is, you're not. You're lying to yourself, performing holiness like a costume you wear over your sin. And one day, the world will strip the excuses away, and you'll be left with nothing but yourself and all the choices you've been pretending weren't yours. That's the lesson to stop pretending, defending, and excusing. Stop asking for change while protecting the very things you need to release. That's not prayer. That's cowardice. And it will cost you everything if you wait too long to face it.

CHAPTER 9:
SEEKING RESTORATION

"But now thus says the LORD, he who created you, O Jacob, he who formed you, O Israel: 'Fear not, for I have redeemed you; I have called you by name, you are mine.'"
- Isaiah 43:1

Deborah Rateree had owned an antique shop on Fulton Street for thirty-seven years. Three decades of handling broken things, chipped porcelain, cracked furniture, tarnished silver, and Faded paintings. Things that other people discarded and deemed worthless because they no longer served their original purpose or no longer maintained their original beauty. Deborah specialized in restoration, not just repair, but restoration. There was a difference, and after thirty-seven years, Deborah understood that difference in her bones. Repair was making something functional again, and on the other hand, restoration was the art of making something whole.

Her shop reflected that philosophy in every quiet corner. It sat tucked into a narrow nook of Fulton Street, easy to miss unless you knew where to look. A small, slightly crooked storefront framed in deep burgundy paint darkened by age and weather, the glass faintly warped so the outside world appeared softened, distorted, slowed before it entered. Inside, the walls were rich with wine-red tones rubbed thin in places by decades of passing hands, the shelves and worktables a worn leather-brown, smooth not from neglect but from care. There were hints of gold everywhere, muted, tired, and honest, catching the light along the edge of an ornate frame or the hinge of an old cabinet, never flashy, never new. Dark greens threaded through the space as well, the mossy velvet of a chair waiting its turn, the patina of oxidized metal, and the quiet suggestion of life clinging to things long past their prime.

Her shop was filled with pieces in various stages of restoration. A Victorian chair with one leg being rebuilt, its other three steady with patience. A grandfather clock missing its face, its exposed interior frozen in silence. A crystal chandelier with half its prisms shattered, light still catching in the fragments that remained. An oil painting so smoke-damaged the subject was barely visible, the past hidden beneath layers of damage but not erased. A music box that hadn't played in fifty years sat open on a corner table, its delicate machinery exposed like a held breath. To most people, these items looked like expensive junk, given their age and origin, but junk nevertheless. Broken beyond saving, too damaged to justify the effort.

But Deborah saw something else. In the hush of the shop, in the filtered light that drifted through the front windows and settled gently on dust motes and unfinished work, the space felt less like a store and more like a sanctuary, a resting place for things waiting to be made whole again. Broken objects weren't judged here; they were studied, understood, and given time.

She saw the maker's mark, the quiet signature left behind by the craftsman who had shaped these pieces when they were new, when they were whole, when they still carried the full intention of the hands that made them. That signature, that mark pressed into wood and metal and glass, that was what made them worth restoring, not their current condition, not their usefulness, not whether they still worked the way they once had or even their beauty as it existed now. But who had made them, the hands had shaped them, the mark they still bore, unchanged by damage, untouched by time. And that, Deborah believed, was what restoration truly meant.

Deborah was seventy-three years old, widowed for eight years, with no children. Her silver hair was always pulled back into a neat bun that revealed the gentle lines of her face, the creases earned from years of attention and care, while her eyes remained sharp and observant, always noticing the small details that others overlooked. She dressed in soft cardigans and well-worn shoes, the kind that had traveled countless streets and held the memory of every step. This shop was her life, the daily practice through which she saw value where others saw only damage. She opened the doors at eight in the morning every day for the last thirty-seven years, except for three days this week, three days since the power had gone out and refused to return, three days since the heavy silence had settled over everything.

Three days since Deborah had woken to find her assistant Shirley gone, her absence marked by a small, uncanny silence that seemed to cling to the corners of the shop, and the evidence of her leaving sprawled across the restoration table behind the counter. The mirror she had been working on the night before, a tall Civil War era piece with a tarnished golden frame and delicate cracks running like spiderwebs across the glass, stood unfinished, a faint smear of polishing cream still lingering where Shirley's hand had passed over it. Beside it her clothes lay strewn as if she had simply vanished mid-motion: a sweater half on the edge of the table, a scarf tangled in the chair, shoes tipped over, a blouse crumpled on the floor, the fabric holding the shape of her body one instant, the memory of her presence the next., as though Shirley had vanished into thin air, leaving only the soft imprint of her presence behind. No note, no word, nothing to explain the sudden absence, just the quiet hum of the shop.

Just like the whispers that had been passing from city to city for weeks, threading through conversation like a cold wind, tales of impossible disappearances, of streets emptied in an instant, of homes left hollow and untouched, and the names carried with them a tremor of inevitability: the Rapture, the trumpet, or the vinyl call. Whatever you called it, the result was always the same: people were taken, lifted, carried away into a quiet brilliance that left nothing behind but absence, while the world continued its slow, indifferent turning, and Deborah remained, still holding her tools, surrounded by fragments of broken things, still trying to restore what might already be beyond repair.

There was a peculiar weight in being left behind, not the sharp sting of shock but the cold acknowledgment that her expectations had never included herself among the chosen, that she had long ago learned the solitude of her own stubborn heart. Her relationship with God had always been complicated, distant, more formal than intimate, like observing a master artist's hand across history without ever being allowed near the studio, allowed only to study, to admire, but never to touch. She believed in Him the way one might believe in a figure whose genius is undeniable, whose work shapes the world, yet who remains fundamentally unknowable, and Deborah had always kept her distance, studying the signature without ever stepping across the line into surrender.

For thirty-seven years she had restored the works of human hands, coaxing beauty back into fractured wood, cracked glass, tarnished metal, while keeping the Divine Craftsman at arm's length, appreciating the world He had made, recognizing His artistry in the careful symmetry of creation, yet never truly offering herself, never truly opening to Him, and now, watching the quiet disappearances unfold around the world, feeling the invisible hand reach and lift, there was an unease that slithered beneath the surface of her steady devotion to craft, a subtle tremor of fear that whispered to her that perhaps even admiration alone might not be enough to protect one from the absence that could come at any moment, leaving only what you hold in your own hands, only what you have not yet surrendered, and the tools and the broken things, and yourself, as the world continues without you.

And now the trumpet had sounded, and she was alone. The shop, once alive with movement and conversation, now held only Deborah and the broken things waiting for her hands. For three days, she had worked anyway, because what else was there to do when the world had shifted and left her behind? The power was out, but the pale wash of natural light spilled through the windows, and her tools did not need electricity.

She returned to the mirror Shirley had been repairing, a magnificent piece from the year eighteen sixty-three, its heavy oak frame carved with careful hands long gone, its beveled glass now shattered, fractured into fragments that no longer reflected a whole face, only broken glimpses, slivers of what had been, a dozen angles of loss and absence.

Shirley had been cleaning, preparing to replace the glass entirely, when the trumpet sounded and time itself ran out, and now only Deborah remained, faced with the fragments and a choice. The simple path would have been replacement, remove the shattered glass, install a new sheet, and make the mirror functional again. Efficient and practical, but Deborah did not repair; she did restoration. Restoration meant honoring what remained, working with the damage, letting it speak, allowing the scars to tell their story rather than erasing them. For three days she had studied those fragments, tracing the edges with careful fingers, imagining a way to restore the mirror without erasing the echoes of what it had been, to let its cracks become part of its beauty, not something to hide or discard, and in that slow, deliberate work, she felt the quiet heartbeat of creation itself, fragile and fractured, yet still insisting on being whole.

It was Thursday afternoon, the fourth day of silence, when a knock sounded at the shop door. Deborah looked up from the mirror, startled, her hands still smudged with polishing cream. She hadn't seen another person since the power went out; the sound of knocking pierced the profound quiet like a ripple across glass. Outside, the world was white and hushed, snow falling steadily, each flake catching the pale winter light and drifting down in slow, silent spirals. The man standing there was middle-aged, bundled in a heavy coat, scarf wrapped tightly around his neck, hat pulled low over his brow, and snow dusting his shoulders. He could have been mistaken for a vagabond, though there was a hunger in his eyes that spoke of wandering, searching, of someone lost.

Deborah unlocked the door and swung it open. The man's eyes met hers, a mixture of relief and desperation shining through the frost and exhaustion. "You're here," he said, his voice rough, as though it had lain unused for days. "I've been walking for hours. Every shop is empty. Every building is locked. But your light was on, and I saw you moving inside. I thought maybe… maybe you could help me."

Deborah smiled softly, brushing a stray lock of silver hair from her face. "Come in," she said, her voice calm, steady. "It's freezing out there. You must be tired from walking in all this snow. Warm yourself by the fire for a moment."

Deborah stepped back to let him in, and the warmth of the shop met him like an embrace, soft and unexpected. The air smelled faintly of polish and wood, of history and careful work. With him inside, the shop no longer felt like a mausoleum of silence but a place where life could still exist. Snowflakes clung to his coat and boots, melting in the heat, as he walked slowly among the tables, running a gloved hand over the broken objects in various stages of restoration, each piece telling a story of care, patience, and quiet perseverance.

His eyes drifted from one object to another, tracing the contours of the chair, lingering on the clock, the chandelier, the painting, before finally settling on the mirror resting on Deborah's work table. The glass was fractured, splintered into countless shards, each reflecting only a fragment of reality.

"You fix broken things?" he said, his voice tentative, almost a statement of awe rather than a question.

"I restore them," Deborah corrected gently, her hands resting lightly on the edge of the table, the words deliberate, careful. "There is a difference."

He nodded slowly, as if he understood, though perhaps he did not, and Deborah did not press him to grasp it fully. He stepped closer, his eyes fixed on the fractured mirror. "Can you… fix that?" he asked, a shadow of hope in his tone, fragile and trembling.

"I can restore it," she said, her voice soft, almost reverent, "but it will never be what it once was. The damage is part of it now, woven into its story. The best I can do is find a way for the brokenness to belong, to become part of something whole rather than vanish into nothing."

He reached out, his fingers trembling as they hovered above the fractured glass, then recoiled, as if the shards themselves carried a truth he could not bear to touch. Barely above a whisper, he spoke again: "Can you… restore people?"

Deborah met his gaze, looking past the surface to the rawness behind his eyes, the desperation, the grief, the fear that he had been left behind while others were taken, the quiet terror that time had moved on while he remained broken, still waiting, still wondering if something could be mended in a soul as fractured as the mirror before her.

"I don't know," Deborah said honestly, her voice soft, carrying the weight of years spent among broken things. "I've never tried. I only know how to restore objects. Pieces. The works of human craftsmen. That's all I've ever known."

"But you said you look for the maker's mark," the man said, his voice trembling, "you said that's what tells you something is worth restoring, the signature of whoever made it. Isn't that right?"

"Yes," she said. "That's the first thing I look for. The mark or signature. The evidence of who created this piece. Because if it was made by a master craftsman, if it bears the signature of someone skilled, then it is worth the effort of restoration, no matter how broken, no matter how fractured."

The man's eyes glistened with tears. He swallowed hard, then tried again, his voice barely more than a whisper. "Do you think… do you think people have a maker's mark?"

Deborah paused, feeling a shift in her chest, a tremor she hadn't expected, a question she had never truly faced. "I don't know," she said again softly, almost to herself.

He pressed on, voice shaking with a fragile hope. "Do you think God's signature… is in us the way a human craftsman leaves theirs on their work? Even in broken people… do you think we still bear it?"

Deborah looked at him, really looked, and for the first time, she wondered not about the objects in her shop, not about the mirrors or the chairs, but about the fragments of human life scattered across the world, and whether they, too, were marked by the same unseen hand that shaped sunsets, trees, and the intricate geometry of a human hand. She thought of Shirley, gone in an instant, and herself, left behind, holding pieces of what she could understand and what she could not.

The man stepped closer to the mirror, his eyes tracing the fractured surface, his own reflection splintered into shards. Each fragment held only a piece of his face, fragments that refused to align, a whole rendered incomplete by damage he could not undo. "I've been walking for three days," he said, his voice low, trembling like the wind outside. "Through empty streets, past abandoned cars and piles of clothes where people used to be. I've been staring at the wreckage and wondering if there's any point in moving forward, if everyone worth saving has already been taken, and all that's left are the pieces too broken to matter."

His fingers hovered for a moment, then touched the glass, tracing the cracks as if he could follow the fractures back to a place where they had once been whole. "But then I saw your shop," he continued, voice catching. "Saw you here, working on this broken mirror, and I thought… if she sees value in something this damaged, if she believes this is worth restoring, maybe there's hope. Maybe broken things aren't automatically worthless. Maybe the damage isn't the end of the story."

He lingered there, fingertips resting lightly on the splintered glass, and for a moment the room felt suspended, caught between what had been shattered and what might yet be made whole, and the quiet weight of possibility hung in the air, fragile as the mirror itself, yet insistent, like light spilling through cracks in a long-closed window.

Deborah stood beside him, and together they looked into the shattered reflection, the fragments catching light in uneven angles, each piece a small, fractured world. And in that moment, a truth she had been circling for three days, dancing around with cautious thought, finally struck her with the weight of inevitability. The mirror wasn't what needed restoration. She was.

All these years, Deborah had been tending to broken things while believing herself whole. She had been a restorer who never considered the need for restoration in her own life, an expert in seeing value in damaged objects while blind to the cracks inside her own heart. She had kept God at arm's length, simply admiring His craftsmanship from afar, marveling at the perfection of His creation, but never surrendering to His authority.

And now she saw it, the truth she had refused to face, she was shattered. Broken into fragments. Like this mirror, this man, every person left behind when the trumpet had sounded, and the whole had been taken home. The realization pressed against her chest like ice. The fear she had kept quiet all these years rose, sharp and insistent. She could feel the urgency of it, the raw, impossible weight of what had been lost and what might still be lost.

"I'm not a restorer. Not really. I mean… I restore objects. I'm skilled at that. I know how to coax beauty back into broken things. But I don't know how to restore myself." Her hands trembled slightly as they hovered over the mirror. "I don't know how to restore you. I don't even know if restoration is possible after… after whatever happened. After missing the call. After being left behind."

The man looked at her with understanding laced with recognition. The look of someone seeing themselves reflected in another person's confession, someone who knew the quiet ache of being left behind.

"My name is Thomas," he said finally, his voice low, deliberate, the weight of years in every syllable. "I used to be a pastor."

Deborah arched an eyebrow, a flicker of disbelief crossing her face. "A pastor? And you… were left behind, too?"

Thomas shook his head slowly, almost mournfully. "I spent twenty-three years preaching about surrender, about letting go, about preparing people for the call and telling my folk they must be ready, must give surrender fully. And when it came… when the call came, I wasn't ready. I was still clinging. Still defending my right to myself. Still believing I could serve without surrendering, that I could guide others while refusing to follow. I thought devotion was a profession, a habit, a practice. I thought faith could be measured in sermons and books and rituals. I was wrong. I was too late."

He turned back to the mirror, his reflection shattered into shards, each fragment catching the light like fragments of his own life. "I've been walking with this weight for days, wondering if there's any hope for people like us, people who thought they knew better and chose worse. People who saw God's signature but turned away, who had every chance to surrender and refused. I've been asking myself if missing the first call means it's gone forever, if the door has closed and locked, leaving only the shame and the fragments of what could have been. And all I can see in the glass is the reflection of my own failure, fractured and incomplete, a life that could have been whole but wasn't."

She looked at the mirror frame again. The beautiful, old cream carved with delicate details, the texture rich and worn with age, and there in the lower right corner, barely visible beneath decades of wear, was the maker's mark. A small symbol, etched with care, a quiet declaration that whispered across the years.

The glass was shattered. Its reflection is broken into a dozen impossible pieces. Its beauty marred and its function compromised, yet the mark remained unchanged. Still claiming and declaring that what I have made is worth restoring, no matter how fractured it has become.

And in that moment, Deborah felt it in herself, a subtle, unshakable truth that even in her own brokenness, even in the fractures of her life and the fragments of her faith, she bore the same mark. She belonged and is claimed. She had always been his.

Deborah's eyes welled with tears, spilling quietly down her cheeks. She reached out and let her fingers brush the maker's mark, tracing the tiny carved symbol as though it could speak to her. "Look," she whispered, her voice trembling, breaking with the weight of realization. "Look at this."

Thomas leaned closer, snow from his coat melting faintly on the floorboards. "The mirror is shattered," she continued, voice catching in her throat. "The glass is broken, so you can't see a clear reflection anymore. And yet… the maker's mark is still here, still etched into the frame, claiming this piece as its own."

He bent closer, eyes tracing the small, careful symbol, the curve and line that had survived a hundred and sixty years. His voice was barely audible, almost a prayer. "Do you think… do you think that's how God sees us? Not looking at the damage, but seeking His signature? Not measuring our brokenness, but recognizing whose we are? Not deciding if we're worth restoring based on our condition, but on the Maker who formed us?"

Deborah could not trust herself to speak at first. She only nodded, the faintest motion, a quiet acknowledgment of a truth she had carried all her life but had never applied to herself. Thirty-seven years she had spent studying maker's marks, seeking the signature that gave a piece value. She restored broken objects not because they were flawless, but because they bore the mark of someone skilled, someone worth honoring. And yet, she had never looked for God's signature on herself. She had never understood that her worth did not depend on her condition, her fractures, or her failures, but on the One who made her.

"I think…" she said slowly, deliberately, choosing each word with care, letting it tremble into the silence between them, "I think that's exactly how He sees us. I think we bear His mark. His signature. The evidence that He made us. And I think that mark… it doesn't vanish just because we're broken, damaged, or because we missed the first call." She lifted her gaze to Thomas, saw the fragile, trembling hope dawning in his eyes.

"I think He specializes in restoration," Deborah continued, her voice steadying with conviction, gaining strength in the quiet. "Not repair. Restoration. Working with the damage instead of discarding it. Integrating our brokenness into something whole instead of replacing us because we are no longer perfect. Every crack, every fracture, every imperfection… it doesn't erase His claim on us. It becomes part of the story He is still writing, the work He is still completing."

Thomas's lips parted, and for a long moment, he said nothing. He simply looked at her, the weight of what she had said sinking in, and in that silence, Deborah felt the room hum with a quiet, almost sacred possibility.

He was crying, the kind of crying that made no sound. Silent tears slipped down his face as he stared into the shattered mirror, his reflection broken into a dozen uneven angles, none of them offering him the mercy of a whole image. And yet the maker's mark remained on the frame, small and steady, still visible, still intact, still declaring ownership despite everything else that had been fractured.

"I've been so angry at myself," Thomas said quietly, his voice thick with regret. "For three days, I've walked these empty streets hating myself for missing it. For not being ready. For spending twenty years preaching surrender while never actually surrendering. For being a professional Christian instead of a disciple." The words seemed to fall out of him, heavy and exhausted, carrying the shame of someone who knew the truth long before he lived it.

Deborah understood the weight of that anger, recognized it for what it was, because she had been carrying the same fury inside herself, sharpened by years of distance and refusal.

"What if," Deborah said quietly, the words forming before she had time to doubt them, "what if the fact that we're still here isn't condemnation at all?" The thought settled into her chest like unexpected warmth. "What if being left behind isn't being abandoned, but being given one more chance, to finally see His signature, to surrender at last to the Craftsman who made us, to stop measuring our worth by our damage and begin seeing ourselves the way He does?"

Thomas looked at her then, really looked, as if something in her voice had shifted the air between them. The fear in his eyes did not vanish, but something else began to rise beside it, fragile and trembling, a hope he had not dared to name. "Do you think there's still time?" he asked softly. "After missing the first call, after proving we weren't ready… do you think He still wants to restore us?"

Deborah walked to her worktable, her movements slow. She picked up her tools, fine brushes, gentle solvents, the patient instruments of restoration she had held thousands of times in her hands. For decades, she had used them to coax beauty back from ruin, yet she had never once turned their lessons inward. And now, as she held them, something sparked in her heart, small but steady, like a flame refusing to be extinguished.

"I think," she said slowly, her voice gaining strength as the truth took shape, "I think God doesn't abandon His work. When a master craftsman signs a piece, that signature is a promise. A commitment. A claim that doesn't expire just because the piece has been damaged." She set the tools down and turned back to Thomas. "I think He looks at us and sees His mark and says, *That's mine. I made that.* And what I make is worth restoring, no matter how broken it becomes."

Her eyes shone now, not with tears alone, but with something brighter. "I think we've been measuring everything wrong. We've been staring at our fractures and deciding we're not worth saving. But God doesn't measure that way. He looks for His signature. And if He finds it, then we are worth every careful, patient act of restoration, regardless of how damaged we are."

Thomas stepped beside her, and together they looked at the shattered mirror, the fractured glass catching the light, the maker's mark still intact, still claiming what had been broken.

"How do we do it?" Thomas asked quietly. "How do we surrender now, after missing the first call, after spending years ignoring His claim?"

She wasn't a theologian or a pastor. She wasn't even particularly religious in the way people usually meant it. She was just a woman who had spent thirty-seven years restoring broken things and was only now beginning to understand that she herself was among them, another fractured piece waiting to be made whole. But one thing she knew how to restore. She knew its patience, honesty, its refusal to rush past the damage, and maybe that knowledge could translate. Maybe the principles that applied to furniture and mirrors and paintings also applied to souls.

"I think," Deborah said slowly, as if listening to the truth form even as she spoke it, "we start by admitting that we're broken. Not defending the damage and not explaining why it's justified. Simply admitting it honestly, that we're shattered, fragmented, and we no longer show a clear reflection." Thomas nodded, something heavy settling in his chest as he saw the damage without the familiar cushion of excuses, without the comfort of explanation.

"And then I think we look for the maker's mark. Not at our fractures, but at His signature. Acknowledging that He made us, that we bear His mark, that we are His work, no matter how broken we've become." She lifted the mirror frame and turned it gently until the maker's mark caught the light, small and unmistakable.

"I think we trust the Restorer. We stop trying to fix ourselves. Stop attempting to replace our own shattered glass. Stop believing we can return ourselves to what we were before the damage. And we surrender to the one Craftsman who knows how to work with broken things, who doesn't discard what's fractured, who specializes in restoration, who sees value not in our condition, but in His signature."

"I see your mark now," she whispered, her voice trembling but certain, "not on the parts of me that are whole, but on the parts that are broken, the places I tried to hide, the fractures I learned to live around. You made me. I am Yours. I carry Your signature even when I no longer recognize myself. And because I am Yours, I stop arguing with the damage and stop pretending I can repair myself. I give You what is shattered, what is incomplete, what no longer reflects clearly, and I trust You not to replace me or discard me, not to turn away in disappointment, but to restore me with the same care You gave when You first signed Your name on my life. Work with what I am, with what has been hurt and worn and cracked by time. Integrate the brokenness instead of erasing it. Finish what You began in me, not because I am whole, but because I am Yours."

The words come to her naturally; they do not feel learned or borrowed but remembered, as though they had been waiting patiently beneath the surface all along.

Deborah felt something loosen in her chest, a quiet release, like a knot finally giving way after being pulled tight for thirty-seven years. It was the belief she had carried without ever questioning it, that she needed to be whole before she could come to God, that she had to repair herself first, polish the cracks, hide the damage, present something acceptable. She had believed brokenness disqualified her. That God must surely prefer those who arrived intact.

But the thought unraveled now, falling apart under its own weight. It was backward. Completely backward. It was like believing she should only welcome flawless pieces into her workshop, like refusing the very things she had devoted her life to restoring. Brokenness was not a barrier to restoration; it was the reason restoration existed. The damage was not the disqualifier; it was the invitation. She had spent her life seeing worth in what others discarded, touching splintered wood and fractured glass and saying, *this can be made whole again.* And suddenly she understood, if that was true of her work, how could it not be true of God's? Why wouldn't He specialize in broken people the way she specialized in broken furniture? Why wouldn't He search for His signature beneath the damage and say, *that's mine. I made that. And I know exactly how to restore it?*

She turned to Thomas, the words pressing against her chest until she had to let them out. "I need to tell you something," she said softly.

He looked at her, attentive, gentle. "I've kept God at arm's length for thirty-seven years," she continued. "I admired His craftsmanship. I noticed His beauty. I respected His work from a safe distance. But I never surrendered. Never acknowledged that if He made me, if I carry His mark, then I'm not mine to fix. I'm His to restore."

Thomas smiled, small and knowing, the kind of smile born from recognition rather than amusement. "Welcome to the club," he said quietly. "The people who admired God from afar while avoiding surrender. The ones who saw His signature everywhere except on themselves. We now finally learn what surrender truly means."

Deborah smiled back, and the weight she had been carrying lifted just enough for hope to breathe. It was the first time she had smiled in four days.

Thomas stepped forward and embraced her. The kind shared by people who had both been brought to their knees and were only now realizing they might not be ruined beyond repair.

They stood there in the quiet, breathing in sync, the weight of shame easing just enough to let hope slip in. Around them in that small human moment, it became clear that their brokenness had not erased the signature they carried.

When they finally pulled apart, Deborah turned back toward her worktable and reached for her tools, the fin,e familiar implements her hands had known for thirty-seven years, tools she had trusted to restore the work of human craftsmen long after time and neglect had done their damage. She hesitated, the weight of them suddenly heavier than usual, and gestured toward the broken objects scattered throughout the shop.

"I don't know if I'm supposed to be doing this anymore," she admitted quietly, her voice threaded with uncertainty as she looked at the fractured chair, the silent clock, the dulled chandelier, the cracked mirror resting on the table. "I don't know if restoring furniture still matters, or if the world has moved on without me leaving this work behind as something obsolete and irrelevant."

Thomas didn't answer right away. He let his gaze travel slowly through the room, taking in the evidence of decades of careful labor, the marks of makers etched into wood and metal signatures pressed into surfaces by hands long gone. Every piece bore damage, but none had been discarded. Every object waited patiently as if trusting that skilled hands would return to finish what had once been begun.

"I think…" he said at last, choosing his words with care, "that your work has always been more than furniture." He stepped closer, his voice steady but softened by something newly understood. "I think you've been practicing restoration all these years so that you would recognize it when you needed it yourself. Every piece you touched, every maker's mark you uncovered beneath layers of damage, every choice to restore instead of replace, I think it was all preparation. Preparation for this moment to finally see that you bear a signature too, and that signature makes you worth restoring, no matter how broken you feel."

Deborah felt the tears rising before she could stop them, and this time she didn't try. They fell freely, landing on the worn surface of the worktable, catching briefly in the grooves of the maker's mark that had survived even as the glass around it had splintered. She pressed her hand to her mouth, steadying herself.

"I've been so afraid," she confessed, the truth spilling out now that it had been named. "Afraid that I wasted my life, that spending thirty-seven years admiring God's work from a distance, instead of surrendering to Him personally, means I missed my chance. Afraid that missing the first call means there isn't a second one, that being left behind means being left permanently, without redemption."

Thomas placed his hand gently on her shoulder, his own voice thick with recognition. "I've been afraid too," he admitted. "Because if a pastor can miss the call, if someone who preached surrender for twenty years never actually lived it, then what hope is there? What possibility of restoration exists for people like us?"

He paused, his gaze drifting back to the mirror, to the small, deliberate symbol carved by a craftsman more than a century earlier. "But then I walked into your shop," he continued, "and I saw what you do. How you search for the maker's mark before you decide anything else, and suddenly I understood what I've been missing all these years. God doesn't measure value by condition; instead measures it by signature. He doesn't decide whether we're worth restoring based on how damaged we are, but on whose we are. And if we bear His mark, if He signed His work, then we are worth every effort of restoration, no matter how shattered we've become."

Deborah nodded, wiping her cheeks before reaching for a fine brush. She dipped it carefully into the solvent and began cleaning around the maker's mark on the mirror's frame, her movements slow and deliberate, revealing the signature more clearly with each pass. She worked as she spoke, letting the truth settle into her hands.

"That's what we need to do," she said softly. "We need to highlight His signature. Make it visible and stop staring at the damage, and start remembering who we are. Stop measuring ourselves by how unbroken we look and start measuring ourselves by our Maker. Stop believing we're beyond restoration and start trusting the Restorer."

For a while, she worked in silence, the brush moving with the practiced patience of someone who had learned long ago that restoration could not be rushed, that bringing broken things back to wholeness required time, skill, and respect for both what they had been and what they could still become. When she finally set the brush down, the maker's mark stood clearly revealed. A small symbol carved one hundred and sixty years earlier by hands whose name had been lost to history, though the signature itself remained quietly claiming ownership".

Deborah looked up at Thomas. "I think we need to pray," she said. "I'm not very good at it. I've talked to God occasionally, but always from a distance, always as an admirer rather than as His work. But I think it's time to pray differently. To pray as someone who bears His signature. As a broken piece surrendering to the Craftsman."

Thomas nodded, understanding now what his years of practiced prayer had never taught him, that God wasn't waiting for eloquence or theology or carefully formed phrases, but for honesty, for the simple admission of brokenness and the trust that the Restorer knew what to do with it.

They knelt together among the broken things, surrounded by objects bearing the marks of their makers, surrounded by evidence that damage did not destroy value and that shattered things could still be restored if someone skilled was willing to do the work.

Deborah spoke first, her voice uncertain and unpolished, the voice of someone praying honestly for the first time.

"God, I don't know how to do this," she whispered. "I've spent my life admiring Your work from a distance, seeing Your signature everywhere, recognizing Your craftsmanship without ever surrendering to You. I never acknowledged that if You made me, if I bear Your mark, then I belong to You."

Her voice broke, but she continued. "I'm broken, shattered… I don't reflect clearly anymore. I missed the call because I never truly surrendered, but today, I understand that my value isn't measured by my condition. It's measured by who I am. So, if I bear Your signature, then I am worth restoring, not because I'm undamaged, but because You don't abandon what You've made."

She took a trembling breath. "I surrender. After thirty-seven years of holding you at arm's length, I admit that I need restoration and that I can't fix myself. I need your hands, skill, and willingness to restore instead of replace. I'm Yours. I bear Your signature, and I trust You to restore me completely, working with my damage instead of erasing it, redeeming what's been broken instead of discarding it."

When she fell silent, the prayer offered and the surrender complete, Thomas prayed next, his words stripped of polish and performance.

"I preached surrender for twenty years," he said quietly. "But I never actually lived it. I talked about it, taught it, and performed it, without ever releasing control. And now I see that I was broken all along, hiding behind language instead of honesty. I see your signature on me now, on Deborah, on everyone who feels left behind and beyond redemption. And I understand that as long as we bear Your mark, we are worth restoring. So I surrender truly and completely, trusting You to do what I could never do for myself."

When they finished, the shop settled into a different kind of silence, not heavy or threatening, but sacred, the quiet of a workshop where restoration had begun. They remained on their knees, not waiting for spectacle, but resting in the reality they had finally acknowledged: they were broken, they bore His mark, and the Maker was faithful to His work.

As the afternoon light faded and shadows lengthened, Deborah lifted the mirror once more, the shattered glass reflecting the room in fragments, the maker's mark still clear and undamaged, claiming ownership, declaring value. And she understood with a certainty that settled deep within her, that broken was not the same as worthless, that damage did not negate worth, and that as long as the signature remained, restoration was always possible.

Because God does not measure value by condition. He measures it by signature. And what He makes, He restores.

I want you to sit with Deborah's story for a moment, with her thirty-seven years of admiring God's craftsmanship from a distance, of recognizing His signature everywhere except on herself. She learned too late,e and then just in time, that value is not measured by condition but by belonging, not by how shattered something is but by whose mark it bears. Deborah restored broken furniture while believing her own brokenness disqualified her, searched for maker's marks on objects while ignoring the Divine signature on her soul. Until a shattered mirror revealed what she had missed all along. Restoration does not begin with fixing the damage; it begins with acknowledging the signature, with recognizing whose work you are, and surrendering to the Craftsman who made you and knows exactly how to make you whole again. You bear His mark even if the damage feels overwhelming, even if you have kept Him at arm's length while admiring His work from afar. That signature is a promise that does not expire with brokenness. Stop measuring your worth by your condition and start measuring it by who you are. The Restorer is waiting, not to replace you or erase what you've been through, but to redeem you, to work with your brokenness, and to make something whole and beautiful because He never abandons what He has made.

CHAPTER 10:
MAKING AMENDS - UNFINISHED BUSINESS

"Therefore, if you are offering your gift at the altar and remember that your brother or sister has something against you, leave your gift there in front of the altar. First go and be reconciled to them; then come and offer your gift."
- Matthew 5:23-24

<u>4 Years Ago</u>

James pushed open the door to his cozy, one-story home in a small town where everyone knew everyone and every neighbor waved hello on Sunday mornings. The walls smelled faintly of polished wood and fresh coffee, and the curtains were light and airy, letting in the soft afternoon sun. The house had a quiet, lived-in warmth, like the embrace of a place meant for family, laughter, and small, simple routines.

Delilah stepped in behind him, smiling, her voice carrying the easy warmth of a shared secret. "I liked the sermon today, Dad. About friendships. It made me think that maybe I should call my school friends later, just to check in."

James chuckled, shrugging off his coat. "That's the spirit. Pastor's right, you know. Friends are like anchors in life. They keep you steady when everything else is spinning."

Delilah leaned against the doorframe. "Maybe you need a friend, too, Dad. Someone to call and tell you not to burn dinner every night."

156

James laughed, shaking his head. "I've got enough trouble right here," he said, ruffling her hair.

Their laughter faded as they stepped into the living room, and the moment of warmth cracked. Samson, his son, was slouched in front of the computer, headset on, shouting at someone on the other end. "Come on! Move! Move! Are you blind?!" His voice echoed sharply, piercing the soft calm of the house.

James' smile faltered. Disappointment burned in his chest. He moved toward Samson, his steps deliberate. Without a word, he yanked the PC cord from the outlet. The screen went black, and Samson jerked upright, eyes wide.

"What the hell, Dad?!" he shouted, rage flashing in his tone.

James' voice was low, measured, but every word carried the weight of hurt and disbelief. "Look at you. Look at yourself. Is this what you've made of your life? You couldn't even bother coming to church today. You call yourself a Christian, where is your faith?"

Samson leaned back, a smirk of nonchalance on his face, though the edge of anger lingered. "It's all pretend, Dad. Man-made rules to scare people. I don't believe in it. You all just need it to feel good about yourselves, to keep yourselves in line. It's a joke."

James' jaw clenched, his anger building. "A joke?" he barked. "You're throwing your life away!"

Samson stood up suddenly, chair clattering behind him, and his shoulders squared. His voice was steady, almost cold. "I'm done with God. Done with faith. I don't believe in it. I'm done."

James froze mid-step, his chest tightening, eyes widening as if he couldn't breathe. The words hit him like a physical blow, and for a moment, he let all his anger come to the surface.

"If you're done… then I don't need a son! I will not have a son who doesn't believe, who has no faith! You can get out! You are not my son anymore! Leave!"

Samson froze, shock and hurt flashing across his face, not expecting the weight of his father's words.

Delilah stepped forward, tentative. "Dad… I think maybe we all need to calm down."

"No!" James roared, voice shaking with raw emotion. "I will not accept a son who has no faith! Who rejects God and everything we believe! You can leave, Samson."

Samson's shoulders slumped slightly, his eyes brimming with hurt, yet a stubborn fire remained. "Fine," his voice low. "I don't need this."

He turned and went to pack his bags. When he came downstairs, he stood paused in front of the door, expecting his father to stop him, but James didn't move. Inside, he felt a strange certainty, a bitter resolve. "He's right. I won't stop him. I won't be proven wrong or made a joke in front of the community. Let him walk out. He'll come crawling back eventually, and when he does, he'll know who's right." James says to himself.

Samson yanks the door open and slams it behind him. The sharp bang made James flinch, a slight, almost unpredictable twitch of his body, and then the house was quiet. The warm sunlight of the afternoon filters in, untouched but colder now, somehow emptier.

<u>Present Day</u>

It had been four years since Samson left. Now James sat alone in his living room at two in the morning. The power had been out for five days. Five days of silence so absolute it felt as though the world itself had stopped breathing. Five days of walking through empty streets, through buildings that once thrummed with life, now hollow and abandoned. Five days of seeing clothes hanging in closets, shoes by doors, dishes in sinks, remnants of people who were no longer there. Understanding with a growing, sinking certainty that something final had happened. The rapture, the trumpet, or the call. Whatever name it bore, the result was the same. People were gone, taken, but he was left behind.

Today, James is fifty-eight years old and divorced for twelve years. He was all alone; his baby girl, Delilah, was taken. He had found her clothes in an apartment three days ago. When he had last seen her two weeks ago, she had been at peace, centered, and grounded in her faith, in a way James had always admired but never quite managed to achieve. She had forgiven him for the divorce, for his shortcomings as a father, and especially for the way he had failed Samson, while trying to appear successful in the eyes of everyone at church.

Delilah was gone, and James missed her with an ache that felt physical. But at least they had reconciled before the end. At least she had known he loved her.

It has been four years, one thousand four hundred and sixty-one days exactly. James had counted. He spent every single day thinking that he should pick up the phone, should drive to Samson's apartment. Should show up on his doorstep and say the words that needed to be said. "I was wrong. I'm sorry. Can't we start over?" but James had been too full of pride to admit he was wrong. Saying sorry wouldn't mean admitting he'd been wrong, which would mean facing the full weight of what he done. How much he'd hurt his son. How did he choose pride over a relationship with his son? He let four years pass in stubborn silence rather than humble himself for thirty seconds of honest conversation.

James replayed that conversation in his mind daily, each word and gesture cut deeper than the last, echoing through the hollow corridors of memory as if the house itself mourned alongside him. He knew he had responded with anger instead of understanding. He gave Samson an ultimatum when what he needed was love. Samson made his choice and walked out the door. It has been four years, and he never returned, four years of sunrises and sunsets measured not in warmth or light, but in the relentless absence of a presence that should have been here.

James spent every day trying to convince himself that he had been right, that he had a responsibility to stand for truth, and he could not simply accept rebellion without consequence. When the truth is that he had chosen pride over his son, chosen the hollow comfort of being right.

Now, time was running out, the trumpet had sounded, and the world had shifted in ways he could barely comprehend. James was left behind with the crushing, undeniable weight of knowing he might never get the chance to speak the words that had haunted him for four long years. Except… Samson might still be here.

The thought had been growing in James's mind for the past 5 days, like a small flame flickering in a room that had long been dark. Samson, the son who had walked away from faith four years ago, who had rejected Christianity, who had turned his back on everything James had tried to teach him… might still be here.

If it was really true and this was the rapture, then the ones taken were the faithful ones, and it was the unfaithful who remained. Those who had walked away, who had turned their backs, were the ones left behind, just as James had been, left to wonder and stumble, trying to understand why they had not been chosen, why they had not been ready.

The possibility had kept James awake for two nights. The fragile, trembling thought that Samson might still be reachable, that the bridge between them might not have been burned completely, that four years of silence might not have to stretch into forever. But there was a problem: Thomas didn't know where Samson lived anymore. He had moved twice since that argument, changed his number, and made himself unreachable. James was so full of pride that he had told himself for years that it was Samson's responsibility to reach out first, that the son who had walked away, who had chosen distance, needed to apologize before forgiveness could ever be possible.

He stood from his chair and moved to the kitchen, the candlelight flickering across the cluttered counters and cabinets. He opens the drawer full of old papers, receipts, and forgotten things that had accumulated over the years. James feels a pang of guilt with every crumpled bill and yellowed receipt, reminding him of time wasted, of moments he hadn't spent where they mattered. Somewhere in the drawer was Samson's old address, written down years ago, a lifeline James had never dared to use.

He sifted through the papers, hands trembling slightly. Bills, tax forms, church bulletins from decades past, each one whispering that he had let the years slip through his fingers. And then a torn scrap of notebook paper, Samson's handwriting scrawled across it, an address from four years ago.

Samson had moved on, but maybe there was a chance, a thin one but a chance nonetheless. It is 2:17 am, and the streets outside are dark, empty, and dangerous. He would have to wait until daylight, but waiting felt unbearable, every second a reminder of bridges burned and words left unspoken. Time was running out, and James could feel its weight pressing down like lead in his chest.

James does something he hasn't done in months. He prays, not the neat formal prayers he recited at church but a prayer that tore itself from his chest, raw and unguarded, spilling from him in ragged gasps and trembling hands pressed to the worn wooden table before him.

"God… I don't know if you're listening. I don't know if I have any right to pray after all this time. After letting pride rule me, after choosing being right over being a father."

His chest tightens as if a fist squeezes around his ribs, stealing his breath. His hands shake, fingers curling into trembling claws. Hot tears stream down his face, stinging and relentless, soaking the sleeves of his shirt and burning the weight of years into his bones.

"But I'm asking anyway. Please, God… let him still be out there. Let me have one chance, just one, to say what I should've said four years ago. Please don't let my stubbornness and my pride be the last word. Please, don't let time have the final say."

Every word feels like pulling thorns from his chest, every plea pressing deep into his belly, his throat raw with desperation. He sobs, leaning forward until his forehead presses to the cool surface of the table, rocking slightly as grief wracks his shoulders and spine.

"I was wrong. I was so wrong. I chose being right over being his father. I chose fear and control over love. I let four years pass in silence, and now I… I don't know if I'll ever get to make this right."

His whole body shakes heavy with the weight of regret, but in the center of it all, in the hollow aching space in his chest, something loosens, a small trembling release, a letting go of defended pride, a quiet surrender he hasn't allowed himself in years. He doesn't feel forgiven or at peace, but he feels light.

James finally stands, his knees ache, and his face is wet with tears, still warm from the confession he has just poured out in the dark of the living room. He looks down at the address in his hand for Samson's old apartment, and for the first time in four years, it feels like more than just a scrap of paper. It feels like a lifeline, a thin thread of hope stretching across the chasm of years and silence, a fragile possibility that his son might still be reachable, that the bridge between them might not yet be burned. James knows he cannot wait until morning, because the urgency presses into his chest with a weight that makes hesitation impossible; every minute of delay feels like choosing pride again.

He grabs his keys, pulls on his jacket, takes the flashlight from the drawer, and walks out into the pre-dawn darkness. The air is heavy and still, the city around him profoundly empty. A haunting reminder of the lives that once filled these streets. He drives slowly, the beam of the flashlight bouncing across the dashboard as he navigates by memory and intuition. Samson's old apartment is across town, normally a twenty-minute drive but James does not know how long it will take now, nor does he care because each rotation of the tires brings him steadily closer to the address on the paper, closer to the possibility of finding his son, closer to the fragile hope of saying what should have been said four years ago.

When he arrives, the apartment complex is exactly as he expected: dark windows staring back like empty eyes, parking spaces vacant and cracked, a profound stillness settling over the building in the same way it has settled over everything else.

James swings open the car door and almost stumbles as he hits the ground. The hallway of the building is silent, hollow, smelling faintly of dust and mildew. He moves quickly, boots echoing against the cracked linoleum floor, eyes scanning numbers on doors, heart hammering in his chest. Apartment two fourteen, Samson's old unit.

The door is closed and the windows dark, but James knocks anyway. The sound was loud and sharp in the empty corridor. A moment passes, and he knocks again. Nothing. He tries the handle, but it's locked. He knocks louder, almost pounding now. "Samson!" he calls loudly, voice trembling, bouncing down the long hallway like a desperate prayer. Nothing.

Frustration and despair press into his chest like a physical weight. The address is useless, a thread that leads nowhere. James turns with shoulders slumped, the flashlight hanging limply at his side, and starts toward the stairs, every step feeling heavier than the last.

A door opens. Not two fourteen, but two sixteen, the apartment next door. James spins, heart, leaping. An older woman stands in the doorway. Maybe in her seventies, with her gray hair pulled back in a loose bun, streaks of white framing a face etched with years of worry and loneliness. Her eyes assessed him carefully, weighing him, the kind of look someone gives when they've been left behind too many times.

"You're looking for the young man who lived next door?" Her voice is rough from disuse yet carries a subtle edge of curiosity.

James swallows hard, stepping closer, his chest tightening, voice thick with urgency. "Yes, Samson Pittman, he's my son. Do you know where I can find him?"

The woman studies him for a long moment, lips pressed together, hands gripping the edge of her doorway. Finally, she speaks, "He moved out two years ago. Bought a house somewhere, I remember him talking about Riverside, near the old mill. Said he wanted space."

James feels a surge of hope burn in his chest. Riverside is only fifteen minutes away. A small neighborhood, maybe thirty houses. He could search, could knock on every door if he had to. If Samson were still there, he could find him.

"Thank you," James says, voice thick, almost breaking. "Thank you so much. I… I don't know what I would have done without you."

The woman nods once, slowly, and James thinks he sees the faintest flicker of recognition in her eyes, as if she understands the weight of a parent searching for a child. Then she speaks again, and her words cut straight through him, a warning as much as advice. "You should hurry. I don't know how much time any of us has left. But if you've got unfinished business… you need to finish it while you still can."

She closes the door. The hallway falls silent again, heavier this time. James exhales sharply, his fingers tightening around the flashlight. Without hesitation, he runs, boots clanging against the floor.

Riverside is quiet, even quieter than the rest of the city. A neighborhood of small houses with big yards, kind of place Samson would have chosen. A place for space, privacy, and distance from the relentless noise of city life. James drives slowly, scanning each house, each driveway, trying to remember what Samson's car looks like, a gray Nissan Rogue? Silver? Blue? He doesn't know, and shame twists in his chest, a sharp reminder that he never bothered to notice.

He turns onto Center Road, and three houses down, a gray sedan parked in a driveway catches his eye. It could be anyone's car, yet hope pulls him forward. Desperation drives his feet as he approaches the small blue house. He knocks on the door, waits, knocks again louder, calling Samson's name. His voice cracks as it echoes down the quiet street, carrying years of fear, hope, and regret.

"Dad?" The voice is tentative, carrying a tremor that James recognizes instantly as his son's. James turns, heart hammering in his chest, and there he is. Older than he remembers, thinner, his beard tracing the sharp line of his jaw, eyes darker, haunted by years James cannot undo. Samson stands in the side yard clutching a flashlight like a lifeline, his posture tense, shoulders slightly hunched as if he is bracing for a collision with the past, or with something he feared might still hurt him.

James swallows hard, tears springing unbidden to his eyes, his lips trembling as the words catch in his throat. "Samson..." His voice cracks on the name, raw and ragged from four years of silence. "You... you're here. You're still here."

Samson steps closer, each movement cautious, as if approaching something fragile, precious, and potentially dangerous all at once. His eyes dart for a moment past James, then settle back, wide and searching. "Yeah," he says, voice low and guarded. "I've been here for five days, trying to... trying to figure out what happened. Trying to understand why everyone's gone. Why I'm still here." He stops a few feet away, the dim predawn light washing over him, casting shadows across his face that make him look both older and younger at the same time. Older in suffering but younger in the vulnerability that he has carried like a wound.

They stand there, frozen in the quiet of the yard. The world around them holding its breath, four years of silence, of missed birthdays, arguments, broken bridges, and stubborn pride pressing into the space between them like an invisible weight. James swallows again, trembling, and finally the words break free, the confession that has lived in his chest for far too long:

"I was wrong. I was so wrong, Samson." His voice shakes, breaking with the effort of speaking years of regret aloud, and his head hangs low. "Four years ago, when I gave you that ultimatum... when I told you that choosing the world over God... when I said walking away from faith was walking away from family... I was wrong. I was terrified, angry, and trying to control something I could never control. And in trying to control you... I hurt you. I pushed you away."

He pauses, his hands gripping the edges of his jacket. Samson doesn't speak, doesn't move, just watches, eyes glistening with unshed tears. James continues, each word spilling like water breaking a dam.

"I should have called you the next day. Should have driven to your apartment and said, I'm sorry. I should have told you that I love you more than I love being right, that you're more important than my pride, that nothing you could ever do or say would make me stop being your father. But I didn't. I let pride keep me silent. I let fear keep me distant. I should have reached out, apologized, and tried to rebuild what I broke, but I didn't. I let the years slip by like sand through my fingers, and all the while… I've been living with the weight of what I've lost, and it has been unbearable."

Tears run freely now, hot and stinging, down his cheeks, soaking into the collar of his jacket, his chest heaving with sobs he has carried alone for years. "I'm sorry, Samson. I'm so sorry for the ultimatum, for choosing pride over you, for letting silence fester where love should have been. I don't deserve forgiveness, I know that. But I'm asking anyway, because I love you, because I've missed you every day, and I cannot bear to spend whatever time we have left with this bridge broken between us."

Samson's chest rises and falls rapidly, his eyes glistening, lips parted as if he's struggling to find the right words. For a moment, the world is nothing but them: the faint glow of the flashlight, the chill in the pre-dawn air, the quiet hum of a city that has stopped, and the sheer, raw weight of a father's regret and a son's withheld grief. Samson steps closer, just a fraction, just enough for James to feel the warmth of his presence, and the air between them seems to tremble with everything left unsaid.

James swallows, tears running into the hollow of his hands as he reaches toward his son, voice breaking again. "Please… let me make this right. Please, let me try, Samson."

And for the first time in four years, Samson's lips quiver, and a single nod passes between them, a silent acknowledgment that the bridge is fragile and trembling, though not yet destroyed.

Samson's shoulders rising and falling as though he were steadying himself against something far heavier, and then he stepped forward, slowly at first, almost hesitantly, before closing the remaining distance and wrapping his arms around his father. Not a quick or tentative embrace, not the kind born of obligation or politeness, but a long, tight holding-on, the kind where bodies lean into each other as if afraid that letting go too soon might undo the courage it took to come this far. His forehead pressed into James's shoulder, his hands gripping the back of his coat as though anchoring himself there, and James's arms closed around him with equal force, palms splayed wide against his son's back, pulling him closer until there was no space left for doubt. It was the kind of hug that spoke where words had failed, that absorbed apology and offered forgiveness all at once, that acknowledged the pain without denying it and chose the relationship anyway, despite everything.

When they eventually pulled apart, both of their faces were wet with tears, both were smiling through the ache of it, and both were changed in a way that felt profound and necessary, like the first truly honest thing either of them had allowed themselves in a very long time.

"I'm sorry too," Samson said at last, his voice rough and unsteady, thick with emotion he no longer tried to hide. He dragged a hand across his face and took a breath, as though bracing himself for the weight of his own confession. "I was angry four years ago. I was hurt, and instead of dealing with it, I shut you out completely. I made it impossible for you to reach me, even if you had tried harder than you already did." His voice wavered, but he pressed on. "And I told myself it was all your fault. I convinced myself that because you gave the ultimatum, you were the one who had to fix it, the one who had to make things right."

He shook his head slowly, shame and clarity crossing his face in equal measure. "But that was my pride talking. My stubbornness and refusal to be the bigger person and reach out first." He wiped at his eyes again, a small, broken laugh escaping him as he exhaled. "I missed you, Dad. I missed you every single day for four years, and I hated myself for it, but I was too proud to admit it. Too afraid to make the first move. Too convinced that I couldn't let you back in until you apologized first." His gaze lifted then, steady and open. "But you're here now. You came. You said you were wrong." His voice softened, filled with something like relief. "And that's everything I needed to hear."

"Tell me," James said quietly, his voice careful, almost reverent, as though he were stepping onto sacred ground. He leaned forward slightly, his hands resting on his knees. "Tell me what these last four years have been like for you. Tell me who you've become. I want to know everything. I want the chance to understand, not to convince you to come back to church, but simply so I can know you. I want to hear your story. I want to be your father in the way I should have been four years ago."

Samson's mouth curved into a smile that carried both gratitude and grief, a soft, weary expression shaped by everything they had lost along the way. He looked down for a moment, rubbing his hands together as if gathering his thoughts before lifting his gaze again. "That's going to take a while," he said gently. "Four years is a lot of ground to cover."

James nodded without hesitation. "We have time," he said. "Whatever time is left, we have it. And I don't want to waste another minute."

They moved together toward the porch and sat side by side on the worn wooden steps. The morning had fully arrived now, the sun climbing higher, the air warming as Samson began to speak. He told his father about the day he walked away from Christianity, about the strange mixture of relief and terror that followed, the way freedom had felt both exhilarating and frightening when he no longer had a script to follow. He spoke of building a life outside the church, of discovering that he could still be kind, honest, and good without religious structure defining him. He talked about the loneliness of severing family ties, the ache of it, and the painful knowledge that it had nonetheless been necessary for his mental health and survival. He told him how he met someone special and fell in love, and they planned a future that felt authentic rather than performed.

James listened. He did not interrupt but simply listened, hearing the man his son had become and the journey he had taken during the years James had been absent. And as Samson spoke, as the sun climbed higher and the warmth of the morning settled around them, a realization began to take shape in James's heart.

His son had not walked away from God; he had simply walked away from the performance of it all.

From a version of faith built on activity instead of authenticity and on appearances instead of honesty. Samson had walked away from the same hollow rituals, the same empty striving, the same substitution of religious behavior for a real relationship with God that James himself should have left behind years ago. And when Samson had dared to be honest about that emptiness, James had punished him for it, because that honesty threatened the carefully constructed image James had spent decades maintaining.

When Samson finally fell silent, James spoke again, his voice low and steady. "I understand now," he said. "Why did you leave. Not just the church, but the faith as we were living it. You saw through something I was still blind to. You recognized that what we were doing wasn't real, that performance isn't the same as surrender, that you can say all the right words and do all the right things and still be completely disconnected from God."

He paused, swallowing hard. "That was me for years. I was a deacon who performed faith instead of living it, who checked boxes instead of pursuing relationships. I cared more about how I looked to others than how I looked to God." His shoulders sagged slightly as the truth settled between them. "And when you left, when you named it as empty, I felt threatened because, if you could see through the performance,e then maybe others could too. I made myself the victim when in reality, I was the one who needed to change."

Samson looked at him with something like wonder, as though he were seeing someone familiar become a stranger and then become familiar again, but altered, softened, more real. "What happened to you, Dad?" he asked quietly. "What changed? Because this honesty and willingness to admit that you were wrong… this isn't the father I knew four years ago."

James drew in a long breath and let it out slowly. "The trumpet sounded," he said, his voice barely above a whisper. "Or something like it. Five days ago, the power went out and never came back. People disappeared." He hesitated, his throat tightening. "Delilah is gone, Samson. I found her clothes in her apartment, but she was gone. A lot of people are gone. The ones who truly surrendered. The ones whose faith was real."

Samson's face drained of color. "Delilah's gone?"

James nodded. "I think so. I think this is the rapture. The end times, and everyone who was ready was taken. Everyone who genuinely surrendered to God. But people like me… people who performed faith instead of living it, were left behind. Given whatever time remains to get honest about who we really are and what we've really been serving."

He turned toward his son, his eyes shining with unshed tears. "And the first thing I had to get honest about was us. This broken bridge. These four years of silence. This unfinished business was eating me alive. I couldn't face whatever comes next without trying to make this right, without saying I'm sorry and asking for forgiveness, even if I don't deserve it. If time is running out, then I need to spend whatever time I have left being your father instead of being right."

Samson sat in silence for a long moment, his mind struggling to hold everything at once: the loss of his sister, the reunion with his father, the possibility that the world as he knew it had ended, and they were among those left behind. He stared out at the quiet street, breathing slowly.

For a long moment, Samson said nothing. His gaze dropped to his hands, clasped tightly together, his thumbs rubbing against each other as if the motion might steady him, and when he finally spoke, his voice was barely above a whisper.

"I wasn't ready either," he said slowly. "I spent four years congratulating myself for leaving the performance behind, for being brave enough to walk away from something empty, for telling myself I had chosen honesty over hypocrisy." He shook his head, a sad self-aware smile flickering briefly across his face before fading. "But the truth is, I never replaced it with anything real. I just walked away. I rejected the fake thing, but I never actually pursued the real one. I never tried to find God outside of church. I never searched for authentic faith, but instead performed religion. I didn't surrender. I didn't seek. I just… left."

He swallowed, his throat working as the weight of the realization settled. "And if what you're saying is true… if the trumpet sounded and people are taken, then I wasn't any more ready than you were."

"We can be ready now," James said quietly, his voice steady but tender. "Both of us together. We can stop performing and finally surrender." He paused, pressing his hand more firmly against Samson's shoulder. "It might be too late for the first call, but maybe there's mercy for people like us, people who are finally willing to admit they were wrong and ask for forgiveness and surrender."

Samson leaned into his father, resting his head briefly against his shoulder. "Yes," he said softly. "Yes, I want that. I don't know how to do it. I don't even know what real surrender looks like, but I want to try with you." His voice thickened.

They remained there for hours, the day slowly unfolding around them. They talked, prayed, cried, and laughed. They remembered the past and grieved the years they had lost.

As the afternoon sun began to descend, James felt something settle inside him that he hadn't felt in years. Peace. Not the false peace of control or the polished calm of someone who looks steady while chaos churns beneath the surface, but real peace. The kind that comes when unfinished business is finally finished.

Four years cannot be erased, and the pain can't be undone, but the bridge was mended. Whatever time they had left, whatever judgment or mercy or reckoning awaited them, they would face it together instead of apart.

James and Samson looked at each other, understanding something profound. Time was running out. They had almost missed it and almost let pride and hurt turn four years into permanence.

Eventually, James rose to his feet, and Samson stood with him. "I love you," James said, his voice muffled against his son's shoulder. "I should have said this four years ago. I should have made sure you knew that nothing you could do or say or believe would ever make me stop loving you. But I'm saying it now that I love you, I'm proud of you, and I'm grateful you gave me the chance to make this right."

"I love you too, Dad," Samson said, his arms tightening around him. "And I forgive you for the ultimatum, the silence, and all of it."

"I forgive you," James said without hesitation. "Completely. No conditions. No reservations."

They stood there as the sun dipped below the horizon, as darkness crept back into a world already changed. James understood the lesson now, the one he wished he had learned four years earlier, the one he hoped others would learn before it was too late. Unfinished business does not stay unfinished forever. Eventually, time runs out.

James had almost waited too long, and the peace that followed was worth every ounce of pride he had to swallow to get there.

Don't wait or assume you have time. Don't believe unfinished business can wait until tomorrow. Tomorrow is not guaranteed. Say the words. Make the call. Mend the bridge. Finish the business.

I want you to sit with James and Samson's story for a second. Picture the weight of four years of silence, the ache of pride, the ache of love left unspoken, and the fragile bridge that nearly collapsed under it all, and then see how it was mended, just in time. The moral of this story is simple but urgent: unfinished business does not wait for your readiness, pride does not pause for convenience, and time is never guaranteed. If there is someone you need to reach, an apology to offer, a bridge to repair, do it now. Speak, forgive, reconcile, and love while you still can, because waiting too long may leave only silence, regret, and bridges that can never be rebuilt.

CHAPTER 11:
DAILY RECKONING AND SURRENDER

"I face death every day—yes, just as surely as I boast about you in Christ Jesus our Lord."
- 1 Corinthians 15:31

Luke Sandoval was thirty-three, a youth pastor at a church that was now empty, and for the past five years, he had dedicated himself to teaching teenagers about radical faith, about dying daily to self, and about the cost of discipleship. On the seventh morning after the blackout, Luke woke with the sobering awareness that he had stopped surrendering. It had not been a conscious rebellion or a deliberate turning away. Still, somewhere between the initial shock of being left behind and the slow, uneasy acceptance of his new reality, he had allowed yesterday's surrender to become today's assumption.

Six days earlier, he had knelt in his apartment, surrounded by darkness and silence, and offered his life to God with a desperation that felt like dying. He had meant every word of that prayer, every tear that fell, every trembling admission that he had been living a performed faith rather than a real one.

Yet after that moment, he had stood up, resumed his routine, and moved through his days as though that single act of surrender would be enough to carry him through whatever came next. He had assumed that one honest confession would sustain him indefinitely. He was wrong.

Now, standing in the quiet aftermath of a world that no longer made sense, Luke understood that what he had once taught so confidently required more than a moment.

He had memorized all the right verses, especially the Gospel of Luke 9:23, which he quoted so often that he no longer needed to think before reciting it: "If anyone would come after Me, let him deny himself, take up his cross daily, and follow Me." He also repeated the words of John the Baptist, "He must increase, but I must decrease," presenting them as the standard for a surrendered life.

The word daily had appeared in his sermons dozens of times. Luke had preached about daily surrender, daily death, and the daily choice of placing God above self. He had explained the discipline of it, the cost of it, and the seriousness of it with clarity and conviction. Yet over time, what he proclaimed had gradually become more theoretical than personal. He spoke of surrender as a concept rather than a consistent practice, as theology rather than biography, as a responsibility his students needed to embrace rather than a command he himself needed to obey with equal urgency.

Until this morning, Luke had followed the same routine he had developed over the past six days. A routine that gave structure to the uncertainty and helped him feel as though he still had some measure of control. He rose from the narrow bed in his apartment and walked first to the window, pushing the curtain aside to check for any visible signs of change in the street below, any movement that suggested restoration or return, but there was none. The neighborhood looked the same as it had the day before, quiet and suspended in an uneasy stillness. He lit a candle because the power remained out, shielding the flame with his hand as it caught the wick, then set it carefully on the counter where it cast a thin, wavering light across the kitchen walls. He assembled the small camp stove he had dug out from the back of his closet, poured in water, and brewed weak coffee from the last of what he had, telling himself that even diluted coffee was still coffee.

He carried the chipped mug to the small kitchen table and sat down, reaching automatically for his journal as he had done every morning since the blackout, intending to outline his thoughts and plan the day. It was in that ordinary, almost mechanical motion that the realization struck him with unexpected force. His hand stopped midway between the table and the journal, fingers hovering in the air as if he had forgotten what he was reaching for. A subtle tightening spread across his chest enough to demand attention, and he felt his breathing shift, growing shallow without his permission.

He had not surrendered today. The thought did not arrive gently; it settled over him with weight and clarity. He had not prayed with desperation. He had not consciously offered his will to God that morning. In fact, he had not even thought about surrendering. He had woken, moved through his routine, and begun planning as though the posture of his heart required no renewal. He realized with uncomfortable precision that he had been operating on the surrender of six days ago, drawing from it as though it were a spiritual reserve he could rely on indefinitely.

His fingers slowly curled inward, withdrawing from the journal, and he leaned back in his chair as the implication unfolded in his mind. Surrender was not a bank account. It was not something he could deposit once and withdraw from forever. It was breath, something that had to be taken in again and again. It required constant renewal, daily practice, and a moment-by-moment choice.

His jaw tightened, and he pressed his lips together, staring at the grain of the wooden tabletop as the realization expanded, exposing what he had somehow overlooked despite five years of preaching about it. If surrender came daily, if the cross was taken up each morning, if dying to self is a continuous practice rather than a single emotional event, then his six-day-old surrender was already six days expired.

A faint heat crept up his neck as conviction settled in. He had been living on spiritual fumes, coasting on the momentum of that first desperate prayer, assuming that because he had meant it once, its sincerity would carry forward without him actively meaning it again today.

Luke pushed his chair back and stood from the table, the scrape of wood against tile louder than usual in the quiet apartment. He ran a hand over his face, pausing with his palm pressed against his forehead as if steadying himself. The room felt smaller than it had moments earlier, the candlelight thinner, the air heavier. What unsettled him most was not ignorance but inconsistency; he knew the truth, had articulated it countless times, and yet he had subtly exempted himself from its daily demand.

He thought about the people who were gone, and the weight of their absence pressed against him with a clarity that felt almost physical. His senior pastor was gone, a man whose quiet discipline had often gone unnoticed because it lacked spectacle. Most of his youth group was gone as well, the very teenagers he had stood before week after week, instructing them about commitment and sacrifice. Others from the church had disappeared too, people who had seemed ordinary in so many ways, yet who must have understood something Luke had missed despite his theological education and his visible ministry position.

They had been ready when the trumpet sounded. The thought unsettled him not because he doubted their faith, but because he had always assumed he stood on equally firm ground. As he replayed conversations and memories in his mind, he began to recognize a pattern he had overlooked before. Their faith had not been built on a single emotional turning point they referenced repeatedly; it had been marked by consistency. They had lived in a state of continual surrender, returning to it quietly and deliberately, rather than relying on a past moment to secure their present.

Luke felt his shoulders tighten as the comparison settled into place. He had checked the surrender box. He had completed the spiritual tasks. He had covered his bases in the ways that were visible and measurable. He had preached, prepared lessons, led small groups, memorized Scripture, and maintained the appearance of devotion. Yet what he was now forced to confront was that surrender was not a box to check. It was a posture to hold and repeat.

The honesty of that admission left him standing still in the dim light of his apartment, aware that what separated him from those who were gone did not have access to the truth, but his willingness to live inside it continuously rather than occasionally.

Luke turned from the window and let his gaze travel slowly across his apartment. The space was small and functional, furnished more out of necessity than intention, and it reflected the life of a man who had spent most of his time invested in ministry rather than in building something personal. The walls were mostly bare except for a framed verse and a calendar still turned to the month before the blackout. The room felt less like a home and more like a waiting area he had occupied between sermons.

He crossed the room to the table, pulled out his Bible, and sat down again, this time with deliberate focus. The thin pages shifted beneath his fingers as he turned to the Gospel of Luke, chapter nine, though he did not need to search carefully because he already knew where the passage was. His eyes found verse twenty-three with ease. He had preached from it so many times that he could have quoted it without looking.

"Then Jesus said to them all, 'If anyone desires to come after Me, let him deny himself, take up his cross daily, and follow Me.'"

Luke exhaled slowly, leaning back in his chair while keeping his eyes fixed on the verse. He had taught this passage countless times, explaining the historical weight of crucifixion, describing what it meant to deny oneself, and urging his students to take their faith seriously. Yet in his own life, the application had gradually narrowed into a single defining moment rather than an ongoing discipline. He had emphasized the drama of surrender without sustaining its rhythm.

It was spiritual breathing, the steady intake of God's will and the deliberate exhale of his own, repeated again and again because it was continuous and necessary. Luke realized with uncomfortable clarity that he had stopped breathing spiritually six days ago. He had taken one deep breath of surrender in that desperate prayer on his apartment floor, and then he had held it, assuming that single act would oxygenate his soul indefinitely.

But no one can hold their breath forever. Eventually, the body demands another inhale, and without it, life begins to fade. In the same way, surrender could not remain suspended in a past moment. It had to be renewed. Without that renewal, something inside him would suffocate, not with the good death of surrender that leads to obedience, but with the quiet, dangerous death of self-sufficiency.

He sat down at his desk and pulled the journal toward him, the familiar weight of it resting heavily in his hands. It was the same notebook where he planned sermons, recorded ministry ideas, and tracked his spiritual life in neat. The handwriting in it was usually steady and structured, bullet points aligned, and thoughts categorized in a way that made growth feel measurable.

He flipped to the last written page, seeing the entry which was dated six days ago, the night of his desperate surrender, the night he had knelt on the floor and finally admitted that he had been performing faith instead of living it. He remembered how intense that moment had felt, how certain he had been that something fundamental had shifted. Yet six days had passed, and there was nothing after it.

The pages that followed were blank. As he stared at them, he understood why. It was not because he had lacked time or because there had been nothing to say; it was because he had grown passive. He had allowed that one emotional encounter to stand in place of daily obedience. It was a lazy spirituality, the kind that speaks confidently about grace but quietly treats it like a blanket that covers you while you sleep rather than a power that confronts and transforms you while you wait. He had been sleeping spiritually, drifting on the memory of conviction instead of responding to it.

Luke swallowed, then lowered his pen to the page. His hand hesitated for a moment before he began to write.

"I have been living off one moment," he wrote, the words uneven compared to his usual script. "I thought because I meant it then, I would automatically mean it now. I had expected yesterday's surrender to protect me from today's pride. I have preached daily dependence while quietly depending on myself."

He paused, his jaw tightening as the admission settled in, then continued.

"I am more concerned with being seen as faithful than with actually being faithful. I know the language of surrender, but I resist its repetition. I want the security of obedience without the cost of choosing it again every morning. I have mistaken knowledge for transformation."

The pen pressed harder against the paper as he finished the thought. There was no outline, no structure, no attempt to make the words inspiring. Only one man acknowledged where he truly stood.

"I surrendered six days ago. I meant it completely in that moment. Every ounce of me, every fear, every plan, every part of my pride… I gave it up. But I haven't surrendered since. I've been living as if that one desperate breath could carry me forever. As if checking the surrender box once makes it permanent."

The words were coming faster now, almost spilling off the page, each one a confession I could no longer hold back.

"I woke up this morning, and my first thought wasn't God. It was my coffee. My comfort. My routine. I've spent six days building a "new normal" in this changed world, and I haven't invited daily surrender into it. I've been managing, calculating, and planning, simply trying to survive. But I guess all of me supposedly died six days ago."

"My hand shivers as I write this. I've been hiding behind the appearance of faith while my heart remains unpracticed and my soul untrained. I am failing, and I am terrified that my knowledge means nothing if I cannot actually live it. I've been pretending to follow, pretending to die, the mirror never lies. I have to start again… Today"

It was as if he were seeing it clearly for the first time in days. His apartment was not just a living space. It was a kingdom. The domain where he was lord. A small, ordered territory, arranged to his liking, managed and controlled according to his preferences. Even here, even in this changed world where most people were gone, and normal life had been suspended, Luke had been quietly building his kingdom. Small, yes, but a kingdom nonetheless. A domain where his will was law, where choices determined outcomes, where he sat in charge.

This, he realized, was the default state of human existence: kingdom-building. Self-enthronement. Crowning yourself lord of whatever territory you could seize. And surrender, true surrender was the abdication of that throne. The tearing down of the walls you'd built. The willingness to be homeless in your own domain, to acknowledge a higher King who already owned everything, including you.

Luke had abdicated six days ago. And then, almost imperceptibly, quietly, he had reclaimed the throne. Rebuilt the walls. Reasserted lordship, not through dramatic proclamations, but in small, insidious choices. Each decision, each subtle preference, had whispered: *My will, not Yours.* Each moment of drift had restored the kingdom he thought he had given away.

He needed a new practice. A new rhythm. Something that would interrupt the slow, quiet pull back to the default. He named it a Daily Reckoning. A ritual of honesty. A deliberate pause to examine the kingdom he had been building, to tear it down again. To stare at the throne he had climbed back onto, and step down willingly. To see the ways his will had risen, subtle and unassuming, and surrender them back to God. Not once. Not occasionally. Every day. Every morning.

It would be daily surrender, alive and breathing, a rhythm of choosing God over self, moment by moment, until the kingdom no longer had a throne and only the King remained.

It was as if he were seeing it clearly for the first time in days. His apartment was not just a living space. It was a kingdom. The domain where he was lord. A small, ordered territory, arranged to his liking, managed and controlled according to his preferences. Even here, even in this changed world where most people were gone, and normal life had been suspended, Luke had been quietly building his kingdom. Small, yes, but a kingdom nonetheless. A domain where his will was law, where choices determined outcomes, where he sat in charge.

This, he realized, was the default state of human existence: kingdom-building. Self-enthronement. Crowning yourself lord of whatever territory you could seize. And surrender, true surrender was the abdication of that throne. The tearing down of the walls you'd built. The willingness to be homeless in your own domain, to acknowledge a higher King who already owned everything, including you.

Luke had abdicated six days ago. And then, he had reclaimed the throne. Rebuilt the walls and reasserted lordship, not through dramatic proclamations, but in small, insidious choices. Each decision, each subtle preference, had whispered: *My will, not Yours.* Each moment of drift had restored the kingdom he thought he had given away.

He needed a new practice. Something that would interrupt the slow, quiet pull back to the default. He named it "Daily Reckoning". A ritual of honesty and a deliberate pause to examine the kingdom he had been building. To stare at the throne, he had climbed back onto and stepped down willingly. To see the ways his will had risen, and surrender them back to God. Not once. Not occasionally. Every day. Every morning.

Luke walked back to his desk with steady resolve and opened his journal to a fresh page. He began to design his "Daily Reckoning". He did not want a ritual he would perform mindlessly, but a framework sturdy enough to hold the weight of daily surrender. It needed to be simple enough to repeat and honest enough to expose him.

Step One: Honest Examination. He would begin by looking back at the previous day without defensiveness. He would examine the choices he had made, the thoughts he had entertained, and the reactions he had justified. This was not about manufacturing guilt or condemning himself; it was about clarity and refusing to blur the truth. He would ask where he had drifted, where he had subtly rebuilt his own kingdom, or if he had climbed back onto the throne without even noticing. The goal was not shame but sight.

Step Two: Specific Confession. He would name what he found. Not vague admissions about being imperfect or flawed, but precise acknowledgment of specific attitudes and decisions. The moment he chose control over trust. The instant his comfort mattered more than obedience. He would write them plainly. No spiritual language to soften or hide behind. He would identify where his will had trumped God's will, where his preferences had outweighed God's purposes.

Step Three: Intentional Surrender. Confession alone was not enough. He would not simply admit his grip; he would release it. For every area exposed, he would consciously place it back into God's hands. If he had clung to control, he would surrender control. If he had guarded comfort, he would surrender comfort. If he had relied on his own reasoning, he would have surrendered his need to understand. This would not be symbolic but deliberate. A choice made again, fresh for that day.

Step Four: Daily Declaration. Finally, he would speak it aloud, not dramatically but clearly. A verbal acknowledgment that he was choosing to die daily, to take up his cross today and follow Jesus. He would not rely on yesterday's sincerity or assume tomorrow's strength. Saying it out loud would anchor it in reality, forcing him to own the commitment rather than merely think it.

Luke leaned back and studied the framework. It was simply a daily practice, the spiritual equivalent of brushing his teeth or making coffee. Ordinary maintenance that, if neglected, allowed decay to set in quietly. The simplicity of it was what made it sustainable.

He closed his eyes briefly and decided he would not wait until tomorrow to begin. He would practice it now.

This morning was day seven, the first day of daily reckoning. Step one, which was the honest examination, and Luke knew this was not about performance but exposure. He closed his eyes and deliberately walked back through the last six days since his initial surrender, since the desperate prayer he had meant completely in the moment.

What had he actually done with that surrender once the intensity faded? How had he lived when no immediate crisis forced him to his knees? Had self quietly reasserted itself while he told himself he was simply being wise.

The answer surfaced faster than he wanted. He had spent enormous energy trying to survive this changed world, calling it rational and practical, convincing himself it was responsible. But underneath the strategy was the need to manage outcomes and to ensure his own safety. Every thought bent subtly toward self-preservation. Every plan assumed he would determine what came next. It was all self-focus. All kingdom building. The opposite of surrender.

He had even been angry, angry at being left behind, angry at himself for missing the call, replaying it with a mixture of regret and accusation. But if he stripped the anger down to its core, there was resentment toward God for the timing, for not giving a clearer warning, for not making the requirements unmistakable.

He had been planning his future, on what to do next, and how to help others. None of those things was wrong in themselves, and that was what made the examination harder, because they carried the appearance of goodness. Yet they flowed from an assumption that he was in charge of his future and that his will shape outcomes.

Six days of gradual drift back to self-lordship. Six days of rebuilding his own kingdom while claiming allegiance to another.

What unsettled him most was not simply that he had drifted, but that part of him had wanted to. Because surrender meant vulnerability, meant releasing authorship, trusting that God's direction might not protect his comfort or his relevance. Beneath all the planning was fear of being powerless.

Step two is a specific confession. Luke did not move from where he stood in the middle of the apartment, the early light stretching thin across the floor, dust suspended in the stillness as if even the air were waiting. The silence felt heavier than before, no longer a place to hide his thoughts but a space that demanded sound, and he understood with sudden clarity that silent repentance had allowed him too much room to soften the truth. Confession needed a voice. It needed breath and vibration and the humility of hearing his own weakness spoken aloud.

His throat tightened before the first word even formed. His hands hovered uncertainly at his sides, fingers flexing as though he were about to steady himself against something solid, but there was nothing to hold except the moment.

"God…"

The word came out rough, barely above a whisper, and he swallowed hard, jaw tightening and eyes stinging as he forced himself not to retreat into thought.

"I confess that I've been trying to control my survival," he said, the sentence trembling at the edges. "I've been trying to manage this situation, trying to make sure I'm safe, trying to build plans that guarantee I won't be caught off guard again." His voice grew uneven, breath catching between phrases. "I keep telling myself it's wisdom, that it's responsibility, but the truth is I don't trust You to carry me through this unless I design the outcome myself."

He pressed a hand to his chest as if the admission had weight. "I've been trusting my ability to figure things out more than I've been trusting You to provide. I've been leaning on my own thinking, strategy, and strength because that feels safer than depending on You when I can't see what You're doing."

The words hung in the air, no longer theoretical. Painful but unmistakably true. His face tightened, and when he spoke again, the vulnerability deepened, the pride he had hidden behind cracking under exposure.

"I've been angry," he said, and the confession came slower now. "Angry at You. Angry at myself. Angry at the circumstances. Angry that I'm here instead of taken. Angry that I missed it." His voice broke slightly on the last sentence, and he closed his eyes, shaking his head as if ashamed of the bitterness still clinging to him. "But underneath that anger is pride. It insists it deserved better treatment. It's me believing I should have been spared, that I should have been clearer, stronger, more ready."

He drew in a shaky breath. "It's self-refusing to accept responsibility. Trying to be a lord instead of a servant. Still trying to negotiate with you instead of bowing."

His shoulders slumped as though the posture of control had finally loosened. He paced a few steps, then stopped again, palms open now instead of clenched, his face flushed with the rawness of saying aloud what he had tried to refine privately.

"I confess that I've been planning my future like it's mine to plan," he continued, voice steadier but softer, stripped of defense. "Like I have control over what comes next. Like my will determines outcomes. I've been living like I'm in charge. Like this is my life to direct." His eyes lifted toward the ceiling, not in accusation this time but in surrendering acknowledgment. "When the whole point of surrender is admitting that you are in charge. That's your life. Your direction. Your will that matters."

His lips trembled slightly, and he let the silence stretch instead of filling it. There was no dramatic collapse, no theatrical display, only the quiet stripping away of illusion. Because you cannot surrender what you refuse to admit you are still holding.

Step three is Intentional surrender. This was the hardest part. The actual releasing, unclenching of fingers that had grown accustomed to gripping control so tightly that letting go felt like stepping off a ledge with no guarantee of ground beneath him. Confession had exposed what he was holding. Surrender required him to open his hands.

Luke stood still in the center of the apartment, morning light now brighter against the walls, revealing the ordinary furniture, everything unchanged, everything indifferent to the spiritual battle unfolding in his chest. His jaw tightened, and his hands curled unconsciously into fists again. He exhaled sharply, bracing himself.

"God…" His voice was lower now, strained, not flowing but pulled from somewhere resistant. "I surrender my survival to You."

The words did not glide out; they scraped. His fingers flexed at his sides, then slowly turned upward, palms open but trembling. "I release my need to control outcomes," he continued, but even as he spoke, he felt the internal recoil, the instinct to qualify the statement, to add a quiet exception, to reserve some corner of authority. "I let go of my planning, my figuring, my attempts to secure my own safety."

He swallowed. "Whatever comes…" The phrase stalled. His eyes shut tightly as fear flared. Images of uncertainty and vulnerability rushed forward, and for a brief second, he wanted to take the sentence back. To soften or even adjust it into something safer.

He forced himself to continue. "Whatever comes, I trust you. Not my wisdom or ability, but only You."

The apartment remained silent. No immediate comfort. He felt the resistance rise sharply then, almost panicked, a voice inside him bargaining to surrender the large abstractions but keep control of the daily decisions, give God the future but manage the present. It would be reasonable. But that was not surrender, that was a transaction.

His breathing grew uneven as he recognized the temptation. "I don't want to let go," he admitted, voice cracking slightly. "Part of me still wants control, even if it is a little. Even something small to manage so I don't feel completely exposed." His shoulders tensed, the honesty costing him. "But that wouldn't be trust. That would be pretending to submit while keeping the final authority."

He drew in a shaky breath and pressed forward, almost against his own will.

"I surrender my anger," he said, more forcefully now, as though speaking over the protests in his mind. "My hurt that I deserved better." His face tightened, and he blinked hard against the sting in his eyes. "I release my right to be upset about being left behind. I accept responsibility for my own choices. For performing faith instead of living it. For teaching surrender without practicing it."

The admission broke something open in him. His voice trembled more visibly now, years of carefully maintained composure thinning.

"I let go of self-defense," he whispered. "Of all the ways I've been trying to protect myself from the consequences of my own failures." His chest rose and fell faster as the dam he had kept reinforced for so long began to crack. "I've been trying to cushion the fall, to explain it to make myself look less responsible. I don't want to do that anymore."

The words began coming quickly and urgently, as though he knew if he paused too long, he would retreat.

"I surrender my plans and my ideas about what comes next." His voice thinned at the edges. "I don't know what tomorrow holds. I don't know if there are more days or if today is the last one. I don't know if I'll survive, or if survival even matters anymore." His hands trembled, fingers slightly shaking. "But I surrender all of it. The future isn't mine… It's Yours."

His lips quivered as he finished, the final words barely steady. "I release my grip on tomorrow… and I trust You with whatever comes."

Silence followed. Luke stood there breathing, hands slowly lowering but not closing, aware that the surrender did not feel triumphant or complete. It felt fragile and incomplete. Something he would have to choose again when fear returned in an hour, or in a minute. Part of him still wanted to grab control back, but he had opened his hands.

Step four finally came, the Daily declaration. This was the seal, the spoken commitment that gave flesh to the internal choice, that made the invisible weight of surrender real in space and sound. Declaring to God that Luke Sandoval was choosing death. He rose from the chair, body stiff, shoulders carrying the invisible bulk of the past six days, of all the planning, anger, and endless grasping.

"Today I take up my cross," he said, the phrase trembling at first, his jaw tight, "Not yesterday's cross or tomorrow's but today. I choose death. Death to my will, my control, and to my kingdom."

The words felt awkward on his tongue, heavy with resistance, and yet each syllable began to loosen something tight inside, something he had gripped for years, a muscle of insistence and self-preservation that did not want to yield. His voice steadied a little, not without doubt, but enough that the internal pull toward reclaiming his throne, toward pretending obedience while quietly holding the reins... faltered.

"Today I follow Jesus," he continued, voice rising and falling with the pulse in his chest, "Not based on yesterday's decision. This morning. This moment. I choose His will over mine. His path over my preferences and His purposes over my plans."

He felt the tension in his shoulders loosen by millimeters, the slight release of a grip he hadn't even realized was still clenched, the subtle exhale of a soul that had been braced for control and now let itself tremble in quiet trust. Not relief in the way a burden disappears, not the triumph of perfect surrender, but the tiniest opening, the faintest hint that letting go could feel like breathing.

He paused, body heavy but somehow lighter in the chest, eyes softening as he spoke the final declaration, the one that made the others possible:

"I am not my own. I was bought at a price. My life isn't mine to direct, and my future isn't mine to control because my will isn't supreme. I belong to You. At this moment, I acknowledge Your lordship. I abdicate my throne, tear down my kingdom, and surrender."

The words lingered, vibrating in the small apartment, not like magic but as the fragile act of choosing once more, the subtle shift of letting go, a space carved open in his chest where grace could enter, where surrender could begin to take root. The weight did not vanish, but softened enough that Luke could finally feel.

Day seven was the day of his First daily reckoning. This wasn't punishment; it was practice. The spiritual discipline that kept surrender real, that prevented drift, that interrupted the slow reclamation of self that happened whenever you stopped actively choosing God's lordship.

Luke stood and walked to his window again. The street outside was silent and empty, the same as the past 6 days, but Luke felt changed simply for today. Because it was this morning and this moment in which he had chosen to surrender. He renewed his death, and that renewal, that daily practice, was the only way to stay ready, because the trumpet could sound again. The final call could come, and the door would close for one final time. When it did, Luke would no longer rely on his past surrender. If there were a tomorrow, he would do it again, and the day after, until the very last day.

Luke walked to his kitchen and poured another cup of coffee. The daily reckoning had taken maybe twenty minutes. It was not an elaborate ritual but simply a focused time.

He thought about his growth group, the students he'd been teaching for five years. How many of them were gone? How many had understood what Luke had missed? But if there were students still here, still left behind like Luke, they needed to know this truth. Not just hear or memorize it, but practice it, live it, and embody it, because hearing about daily surrender would not prepare them for the next call any more than hearing about daily surrender had prepared Luke for the first call. They needed to practice, to develop the discipline, and to make daily reckoning part of their routine.

Luke decided he would write about this, not as a sermon, lecture, or guide, but as a practical framework for daily surrender. Something concrete others could use. Not necessarily his framework, each person would need to develop their own practice, and he will simply provide them with a starting point. Sort of like a template, an example of what daily reckoning could look like.

He sat back at his desk and began to write, not in his journal now but on fresh paper. Clear instructions and practical steps to the framework of *"Daily Reckoning: A Practice of Continuous Surrender."*

Luke wrote quickly, thoughts flowing, five years of teaching about surrender finally crystallizing into practical application. Not theory anymore, but finally something practical. The discipline he'd just discovered and knew he would need to repeat. He explained the *why* before the *how*: why daily reckoning mattered, flexible enough to adapt but structured enough to follow, a skeleton each person could flesh out with their own specifics.

Luke wrote for an hour, maybe more. When he finished, he had several pages. A practical tool for the discipline of daily surrender. Something he could share if he found others, teach if there were still students to teach, but more importantly, something he could practice himself. Tomorrow and every day after that until his last day on earth.

He walked to his small closet and pulled out his backpack, the one he used for youth group trips, and carefully placed the pages about daily reckoning inside. Ready to share if he found others, or ready to reference himself when he needed a reminder of why this practice mattered.

Then he knelt. Not for a long, dramatic prayer, but for simple recommitment, sealing the morning's reckoning, acknowledging that the choice made hours ago would need to be made again tomorrow.

"Thank you for showing me my drift. Thank you for the uncomfortable recognition that I've been coasting on yesterday's surrender. Thank You for the gift of daily reckoning, of continuous choice, of participatory grace. Help me practice this tomorrow, and the day after, and every day that remains. Keep me surrendered, please, so I can die daily. I will stay ready, not through my strength, but through choosing Your lordship continually. Today I choose You. Tomorrow, I will choose you again, and that's my preparation.

That's my readiness, my surrender. Not once but daily. Thank you for making it possible. For inviting me to participate. For giving me the practice that keeps surrender real. Amen."

Luke stood. The day was beginning properly now, seven hours late by conventional standards, but right on time for spiritual reality. Tomorrow he would have to do it again, and that wasn't a burden; it was a gift. The daily invitation to choose and the continuous opportunity to die. The repeated chance to surrender as many times as needed. Daily, until daily wasn't needed anymore because the final call had come, and readiness was tested. But today, Luke was ready.

He sipped his coffee and looked around his apartment with new eyes. This wasn't his kingdom anymore or a domain under his control; it was borrowed space, a temporary lodging, a place where he lived but didn't rule, where he stayed but didn't reign, because he had surrendered.

I want you to sit with Luke's story for a while and realize that the Daily Reckoning is not a burden, but a gift. Not punishment, but preparation. Not a requirement for earning God's favor, but a practice for maintaining surrender to God's lordship. Luke had discovered it seven days too late to be taken in the first call, but not too late to be ready for whatever came next. And that readiness, born from daily dying, maintained through daily reckoning and lived through daily surrender, was all Luke had to offer. Not past righteousness, accumulated spiritual credentials, or years of ministry or theological education. Just today's surrender. Fresh, new, and active.

CHAPTER 12:
THE POWER OF "ONLY": A SINGLE PRAYER THAT CHANGES EVERYTHING.

"Whom have I in heaven but you? And earth has nothing I desire besides you." - **Psalms 73:25**

Timothy Powell had run out of words three hours ago. He sat in the hard plastic chair beside his mother's hospital bed, holding her hand, watching the shallow rise and fall of her chest. His mind was empty of prayers and everything except the raw and unrelenting awareness that she was slipping away, and there was nothing left within his power to stop it.

The hospital room around them felt less like a place of healing and more like a quiet waiting chamber where hope had thinned to something transparent and fragile. The walls were painted in a color that might once have been called cream but now seemed closer to a tired gray under the hum of fluorescent lights that cast a pale, unforgiving glare across every surface. The air carried the sharp scent of antiseptic layered over something metallic and faintly stale, as though even the oxygen circulating through the vents had passed through too many lungs before reaching this room. The blinds were half-tilted over a narrow window, allowing in a diluted strip of winter light that did little to warm the space.

Timothy looked as though the hours had carved themselves directly into his face. His dark hair, once kept neatly trimmed, had grown uneven at the edges, and strands of gray threaded through it in a way that spoke less of age and more of accumulated strain. A day's worth of stubble shadowed his jaw, and the skin beneath his eyes bore deep crescents of fatigue that no amount of rest could have erased in this moment. His shoulders, broad and once carried with quiet confidence, now curved inward slightly as though bracing against an invisible weight, and his shirt, wrinkled from long hours in the same position, hung loosely against a frame that had lost some of its solidity in recent months. His hand enveloped his mother's fragile one, his thumb moving unconsciously back and forth across her papery skin, memorizing its texture, as though touch might anchor her here a little longer.

His mother seemed diminished by the bed that held her. Her cheeks had hollowed; her once warm complexion reduced to a pale translucence through which faint blue veins traced delicate lines. Her lips were dry and slightly parted, and each breath she drew sounded shallow, uneven, as though her lungs were negotiating every inhale.

The power had been out for nine days, nine days since the blackout, since the silence descended and settled over the city like ash. The world had shifted so violently that most people had simply vanished, while Timothy found himself still here, left behind with a reality that felt less like survival and more like judgment. The hospital, once alive with movement and layered with the ordinary noise of humanity, had become a hauntingly depressing shell of its former self. The overhead lights flickered with a weak, inconsistent glow that cast long, distorted shadows down corridors now stripped of urgency, as though the building itself understood that it was failing. The staff had been reduced to three nurses and one exhausted doctor for the entire structure, their faces drawn tight with fatigue and something close to resignation, moving through the hallways with the subdued caution of people who no longer believed reinforcements were coming.

Most of the patients were gone, leaving behind empty beds with rumpled sheets that still bore the faint impressions of bodies that would never return. Yet his mother remained in room four seventeen, unconscious and fading, her body losing its battle against pneumonia that had spiraled into sepsis because there were not enough antibiotics left in a system that had collapsed along with everything else. The very institution designed to save her had become another casualty of the unraveling world, and Timothy could feel the bitter irony of it pressing against his ribs as he stood in that failing building, surrounded by the hollow quiet of a place that no longer promised healing, only delay.

Timothy is forty-one and divorced. Once a man whose life had felt neatly arranged in spreadsheets and schedules, running a software company that now existed only in memory, its walls and promises gone along with the clients and contracts he had once managed with quiet pride. No children had tied him to the future, and the solitude of his existence had once been a choice, but now it pressed in on him, sharp and unrelenting, as he sat beside the woman who had spent her life praying for him, watching helplessly as she slipped away.

For three hours, he had been praying… or trying to pray. The words that had once carried meaning now emerged from his lips as if mechanically, like lines memorized rather than felt from the heart. He recited every prayer he had ever learned, every verse he had memorized as a child in Sunday school, every spiritual formula and phrase, every carefully constructed incantation he could dredge up: *"Heal her". "Save her". "Please God, just let her live. Give her more time. Work a miracle. Show your power. Demonstrate your love. Don't take her. Not now. Not like this."*

At first, the words tumbled out with a desperate clarity, the tone of someone trying to order the universe, to bend fate with faith alone. But as the minutes bled into hours, the recitations became hollow echoes of themselves, the cadence more automatic than heartfelt. Not because he had given up, but because he had run out of language.

In the oppressive silence that followed, Timothy sat holding his mother's hand, feeling the weight of it all settle like a stone in his chest. She had been unconscious for two days. The doctor had said it was a matter of hours, maybe a day at most. Her body was shutting down. Without proper medical intervention, antibiotics, or equipment, she would die. For the first time, the realization sank fully into him physically, as if the very air pressed against his lungs; there was nothing he could do to save her.

Timothy's mom was seventy-six years old. Joyce Powell, her friends called her Joyce Ann with love. A woman of simple faith and profound kindness who had spent her entire life believing in a God Timothy had only recently begun to wonder might actually exist. Timothy always thought of her faith as quiet, nothing dramatic or performative. She didn't lead Bible studies, didn't teach Sunday school, or serve on church committees. She simply prayed every morning without fail. Simple prayers are almost like having a conversation with God. She spoke to Him as if He were sitting in the room with her.

His mother's faith had always seemed naive to him, almost childlike. The kind of simple belief that worked for people who didn't think too critically about theology, or confront the harsh realities of a world that so often seemed indifferent to suffering. She never wavered, never doubted, never complicated her faith with intellectual gymnastics. She simply believed completely that God was real and could be trusted even when everything around suggested otherwise. Timothy remembered his mom with a flicker of warmth spreading in his chest, a little joy in the memory of her voice. And then it came… the weight of inevitable sorrow pressing down that she was dying.

Timothy knew the Bible from his time spent with a youth group. He remembered sitting in a crowded church basement, memorizing verses and listening to his peers speak of faith and purpose. He had even gone on mission trips in college, traveling with groups of students to communities he barely understood, performing tasks he was told were meaningful. But it had all been done actively, without any real relationship. Full surrender had always felt too risky and frightening to him, as if yielding himself completely would leave him exposed to forces he couldn't control.

He looked at his mother's face, now pale and drawn. The face he had known his entire life, but had never truly seen until now, until the sharp edge of mortality made every fine line vivid. He saw the small crease where she always smiled at him, and he realized how much he had taken her for granted. How many conversations he had rushed through, how many visits he had cut short, how often he had been too caught up in his own life to really be present in hers.

She had never complained, never demanded more of his time, or made him feel guilty for living his life in the way he wanted. She had only loved and prayed for him. She was the only one who believed in him, even on days when he didn't believe in himself.

All he had ever really had was her, and the fear of losing her, of being left alone in the quiet aftermath of her absence, tightened around him like a vice. Timothy felt like his heart was breaking open… but it was too late.

Her skin was paper-thin, cool to the touch. She was too far gone, teetering on the edge of whatever lay beyond, the boundary between life and death dissolving like mist around her fragile body. The transition had begun, subtle and unstoppable, pulling her away from him in increments so small and quiet that he could almost pretend she was still here. Almost.

He wanted to pray. Needed to pray. But the words had deserted him, leaving only the hollow echo of his own voice, exhausted from three hours of pleading, bargaining, begging, and bleeding out every form of request he could summon. None of it had worked. None of it had changed a thing. She was still slipping away, and God was still silent. Timothy was left clutching a hand that had given him everything, watching helplessly as the one person who had always put him first began to drift beyond his reach, toward a place he could not follow.

What prayer remains when every prayer feels like it has bounced off the ceiling and fallen back down, unanswered and meaningless against the enormity of what is happening? What words suffice when words themselves seem hollow, incapable of reaching the place where the truth of your fear lives? Timothy didn't know. He just sat there, slumped in the hard plastic chair, holding his mother's hand, her fingers limp beneath his, feeling the slow, inexorable slip of life from her body as if it were draining out into the air around them.

The weight of his helplessness pressed down on him like a physical force, crushing his chest, making it almost impossible to breathe, almost impossible to think. His shoulders shook. He didn't even realize the first tear had slipped from the corner of his eye, tracking down the side of his face, hot and shameful, tasting of everything he had tried and failed to do.

And then, from somewhere so deep inside, from a place he didn't even know existed, the words came, trembling and fragile, breaking out of the despair that had pinned him to that chair like chains. Not eloquent, not even a complete thought. Just a single, trembling cry, a whisper that felt as though it had been dragged from the marrow of his bones.

"Lord Jesus."

He barely heard it himself, barely forced the sound past his lips, rough and broken, ragged with exhaustion and grief. A sound like pleading and surrender wrapped into one. Just the name. Not a prayer in any formal sense. The name his mother had spoken every day of her life, the first word on her lips in the morning, the last at night, and the name that had always been enough to carry her through. Now, in his moment of utter helplessness, it was all he could say. "Lord Jesus."

Timothy sat with those two words and let them linger in the fragile air of the hospital room, as though it was something living, something sacred. This felt different. The prayers he had been forcing from his lips for the past three hours had been crowded with urgency and demand, filled with what Timothy wanted. They had carried the sharp edge of desperation, the subtle insistence that heaven bend toward his will, that the outcome change because he could not bear it otherwise. Those prayers had been saturated with his fear, and his frantic attempt to regain control over a reality that had already slipped beyond his grasp. They had been loud with his own name echoing beneath them.

But these two words were stripped of all of that. These words did not ask. They did not negotiate or bargain. This was simply a surrender wrapped inside a name. In speaking his name, Timothy felt something in him loosen, something unclench that he had not realized had been wound tight for decades. For the first time that night, he was not trying to direct the story. He was not trying to seize the pen from God's hand but simply naming the One who held it.

Another word rose within him, fragile and hesitant at first, yet carrying a weight that shifted everything inside his chest. A single word that transformed acknowledgment into surrender, that turned recognition into relinquishment. "Lord Jesus… only."

Three words, and yet they seemed to contain more truth than all the desperate paragraphs he had poured into the silence for hours. It was the shortest prayer Timothy had ever prayed, the simplest, and it was also the most honest thing that had ever left his lips. In that small trembling addition, something decisive happened within him. He was no longer merely naming Christ; he was yielding to Him.

"Lord Jesus, only You."

That was the bedrock truth beneath all his pleading, beneath every frantic request and bargain and argument he had attempted to construct in order to bend reality to his will. There was only Jesus. Only His power and authority. Timothy felt the illusion of shared control collapse in that moment. It was not the doctors who held his mother's life, not the dwindling medicine supply, or human knowledge that could tip the balance between life and death. Even the systems that had once promised security had proven fragile. The source had always been the One to whom she prayed, the One she loved.

The prayer hung in the air of the hospital room, four words and sixteen letters, yet somehow carrying the full weight of everything Timothy had been trying to articulate for the past three hours. In those words was the essence of every prayer he had memorized as a child, the core of the Gospel he had heard preached countless times but never truly understood until this moment, when the sterile brightness of the room and the fragile rhythm of the machines stripped away every illusion of control he had been clinging to.

For the first time, Timothy understood that truth did not need embellishment. Jesus was not one of many. He was the foundation itself, the only one. Everything else Timothy had trusted in, plans, health, stability, and his own strength, had always been subject to change and vulnerable to fracture.

Timothy had spent forty-one years building his life on sand, on his own intelligence, his own relentless ability to figure things out and make things work. For decades, it had seemed to hold. The structure stood, and the days unfolded predictably. The storms either passed him by or remained distant enough to ignore.

But when the real storm came, and the power went out, when the world shifted beneath his feet, and his mother began slipping toward death, his foundation began to crumble. The strategies that had always rescued him offered no rescue. The confidence that had once steadied him now felt thin, almost hollow, because it had always been sand. Sand that felt solid as long as the skies were clear, but sand nonetheless.

When every effort, logic, and strength failed, only Jesus remained. Not as a last resort in a list of options, but as the only thing that had never depended on Timothy's ability to maintain it.

Tears ran unbidden down his face, and his voice caught as he finally tried to speak. "Only You… only You…" His lips quivered, his jaw tightened, and the sound of his own voice breaking made him flinch, but he could not stop. He could only pray, stumbling over the syllables, voice breaking into quiet sobs, until it became a rhythm he could no longer control.

"Only You. Only you can heal her. Only you can give her more time. Only You can work a miracle. Only you decide. Only You have authority. Only You, my God."

The prayer was a complete surrender. Not of hope, but of control. Not of love, but of illusion. Not of faith, but of pretense that he had ever truly held the strings. Only Jesus. Only Jesus was the rock, and he was enough when everything else crumbled.

Finally, he stopped fighting it and let himself fall into the truth he had been avoiding for years. "Lord Jesus… Only You." The words trembled on his lips, broken and jagged, raw with hope and surrender.

The tears came flooding over him, running down his face, soaking into the collar of his shirt, pooling in his hands where they gripped the sheets as if letting go could somehow be held. Tears that carried years of pretending, years of control, and believing he could manage life with his own hands. Now he was letting go of finally admitting the truth he had always known but had never faced. The cry itself became prayer, until every broken sound of him gave way to the simplest, most complete truth he had ever spoken, "Only You. Only You."

Nothing was required beyond Jesus Himself, nothing Timothy could add. There was no calculation or clever phrasing, simply complete and unflinching surrender. The acknowledgment that Jesus was sufficient, that Timothy was not. Jesus was enough, and nothing else could or should fill that void.

"Lord Jesus. Only You." Timothy whispered it again and again, his voice raw, cracking under the weight of its truth. Not because repeating the words could coax a miracle or make God bend to his will, or because repetition offered magic, but because each repetition was a layer of release, a peeling back of control, until all that remained was the pure recognition of who was God and who was not.

The prayer was short, capable of being spoken over and over without pause, yet infinite in depth: "Lord Jesus. Only You." The entirety of all his fears, hopes, and all his desperate attempts at control fit into these four words. The authority above every authority. The power above every power. Timothy let every ounce of himself fall away, finally understood that the world could collapse, that life could fail him, and still he would have everything, because Jesus was enough.

"You can give her more time, I can't. I have no power, no authority, or ability. I've tried everything. Said and done everything, but it's not enough. I'm not enough, only You are enough."

Every thought and every attempt to negotiate with life itself, the words he had spent three hours crafting, collapsed in his mind, like sand slipping through fingers.

There were no right words. No formula, clever argument, or strategy could bend eternity. There was only surrender. Only the raw, trembling acknowledgment that Jesus was God and Timothy was not, that Jesus had power and he did not, that only Jesus could do what needed to be done, and that his only choice was to trust, to let go, and release himself from the illusion of control.

"Only You. Not my will, but Yours. Not my timing, but Yours. Not my plan, but Yours. Only Your authority. I surrender and release myself. I trust… only You."

The words spilling past his lips with a tremble, tearing through the weight that had lodged in his chest for hours. His body shook from the force of it, from the years of trying to carry everything alone, finally giving way, and he let himself weep, finally weep, feeling the raw vulnerability of the moment press into him. It was emptying, but not despairing. Empty like a vessel that had been filled with itself and was now open, hollow, ready to receive something greater. Empty like surrender always feels, frightening and freeing all at once.

His mother's breathing shifted to shallower now, each inhale a little more laborious than the last. The doctor had said this would happen, the final transition from life to death, the moment when the body begins to release its hold and the spirit prepares to depart. Timothy leaned closer, pressing her hand to his chest, whispering near her ear, though he didn't know if she could hear him.

"Mom… I'm here. I'm right here. And Jesus is here too. The One you've trusted your whole life… He's here. You can let go now and go to Him. He can take you home."

The words trembled in his throat, faltering, yet somehow, they felt right. He was not trying to hold her here against her own time, but releasing her and finally letting go. Entrusting her to the only One who could guide her safely through what he could not enter.

"Lord Jesus… only You can take her home. Only You know the right moment. Only You can guide her through the valley. I can't go with her. I can't do anything… except trust You. I trust You with her, with this moment, with everything… only You."

Finally, after years, he was letting go, not just of his mother, but of the illusion that he had control over life or death.

In that release, Timothy felt a lightness in his chest, a hollow space that had once been clenched with fear and helplessness now empty and ready to trust. His mother was going to the best of places; that knowledge and surrender filled him with an unexpected peace. His sobs now softened. His heart was beating in rhythm with the faith he had finally embraced.

Timothy washed her face slowly, memorizing every line that had carried a lifetime of love. He said goodbye without words because there were none adequate for this moment—no phrase that could hold the weight of what goodbye meant. Only the quiet witness of being here and holding her hand, letting her know she was not alone as she made the transition from this life to the next.

And in those final moments, Timothy's heart spoke the only prayer that mattered, the only prayer that cut through all the religious language to reach the essential truth, "Lord Jesus, take her home. Receive her spirit and welcome her into Your presence. She has trusted You her whole life; now she is trusting You with her death. So I release her to You completely. I'm letting her go now, she has always been Yours."

Joyce, Ann Powell, took her last breath at four thirty-seven in the afternoon on the ninth day of the blackout. Without drama or struggle, just the final exhale. The heart that had carried her life since before Timothy was born ceased its rhythm; this woman he called Mom was no longer gone. Her body remained warm and familiar, her hand still in his, but she was gone. The essence and spark that had made her who she was had left. Moving to wherever spirits go when their time on earth is done.

Timothy held her hand and prayed, "Thank you for being with her. For receiving her spirit. To prove that death is not the end, that You are Lord over life and death. Only You conquered death; therefore, only You can carry us through it. Thank you for being all that she ever needed."

The nurse came quietly and checked her pulse, noted the time of death, and asked if he wanted a few more minutes. He nodded and she left without a word. Timothy stayed, not because he thought she was still here, he knew she wasn't but because he needed to sit with the truth of what had just happened. The awakening in his own heart.

He pressed her hand to his chest one last time, feeling the hollow space left behind, yet strangely filled with peace. She was somewhere else now, somewhere he could not yet go; he knew only Jesus could carry her safely, and because of that, Timothy could release her without despair.

Timothy left the room slowly, walking down the quiet hospital corridor past empty rooms, and the lingering traces of a healthcare system that had done its best but could not save everyone. His mother was gone, and Timothy felt different. Not because the circumstances had changed, she was still dead, the world still broken, but because he had shifted his foundation. His faith, once theoretical, had become real.

That was the power of *Only*. It transformed scarcity into abundance because when Jesus was all you had, you had all you needed. When Jesus was the only foundation, you had the only foundation that mattered. Timothy carried that truth with him as he reached his apartment, the ninth sunset since the world had changed, painting the city in muted gold. He climbed the stairs to his fourth-floor unit and stepped inside to the quiet emptiness of his small apartment, but it didn't feel empty now. It felt different... he felt different.

The power outage still held the city in its dim, and the world outside was still broken. Everything externally was the same, but internally, Timothy was transformed. He moved to his small kitchen table, lit a candle, and let the flickering warmth settle over him. The light trembled across the wall,s and he breathed deeply, feeling the weight of grief, surrender, and revelation all at once.

He pulled a piece of paper and a pen toward him. He needed to write this down, not for anyone else, but for himself, for remembering and capturing what had been etched into his soul in the hospital room. One final, fleeting chance to cement it before the world pressed in again. He wrote at the top of the page: *The Prayer of Only*.

The words flowed, straight from the marrow of his experience, crystallizing insight he could finally name, "When I ran out of words at my mother's bedside, I found the only words that mattered were *Lord Jesus, only You*. Four words that contain everything. The whole Gospel in miniature. Complete faith in concentrated form. Jesus is Lord, not a historical figure, but Lord. Master and King. The One who has power over everything, including life and death. This prayer strips away all the additions; all the ways I try to supplement Jesus. Only means there is nothing to add. Nothing is required beyond Jesus Himself. Nothing I can contribute that makes Jesus more sufficient."

Timothy paused, staring at the page. The words weren't just ideas anymore; they had settled into his bones. This was the foundation he had been missing his entire life, and when the trumpet sounded, when the faithful were taken, and the performers were left behind, his mother would be ready, because her foundation had always been rock.

He continued writing, the pen almost moving on its own, tracing the truth he had lived through grief and helplessness.

"I've spent forty-one years trying to be sufficient, trying to be enough, trying to handle life with my own intelligence, effort, and capability. But when my mother was dying, and I was powerless, I finally understood that I am not sufficient, never was, and never will be. Only Jesus is sufficient. That's not pessimism about human capability; it's realism about human limits. We were never meant to be our own saviors. Never meant to be our own source. Never meant to be sufficient in ourselves. We were meant to depend and surrender to the only One who is actually sufficient. *Lord Jesus, only You.* This is the prayer I will pray from now on. Not only when I'm desperate or when I've exhausted every other option, but because it is the truest and most honest prayer that acknowledges reality rather than attempting to create my own."

He folded the paper carefully, placing it in his pocket. His mother's death certificate went into the other. Two documents: one marking the end of her life, the other marking the beginning of his new understanding. Both connected, both flowing from the same truth.

Timothy understood now that he was not the hero of his own story. He was not sufficient in himself. He could not save, could not fix, could not hold life together alone. Only Jesus was sufficient. Only Jesus was the hero and savior. His story was about learning to trust, not to fight, to yield, not to manipulate. To stop trying to control the uncontrollable and rest in what was real.

He blew out the candle and sat in the darkness of his apartment. The shadows stretched along the walls, quiet and still, yet not empty, not oppressive. It was the quiet of sacred space, the hush of prayer lived, the stillness of surrender. The apartment, the city, the world, all broken, but Timothy had found the foundation that could never be broken, *Lord Jesus.*

I want you to sit with Timothy's story for a while, because in some way or another, you have been there too. Praying elaborate prayers, searching for the perfect words, arranging syllables like levers to move God, exhausting yourself with effort, eloquence, and religious vocabulary, all while missing the simple and unshakable truth beneath it all, four words, the power of *Only.* The prayer of complete surrender, the acknowledgment that Jesus is everything and you are not, the foundation that holds when everything else crumbles, the rock that stands when every strategy, every plan, every effort proves to be sand. This is the sound of *Only,* the prayer that prepares you for the final trumpet, the call that pierces through all illusions, the voice that commands, the moment when only those who trusted solely in Jesus will hear and respond, because only Jesus is Lord, only Jesus holds power, only Jesus is enough. "Lord Jesus, only You." Today, tomorrow, and every day until the trumpet sounds. That is the prayer and the only foundation that will never fail. Only Jesus.

CHAPTER 13:
THE ROMANS ROAD

"He who testifies to these things says, 'Yes, I am coming soon."Amen. Come, Lord Jesus. The grace of the Lord Jesus be with God's people. Amen."
- **Revelation 22:20,21**

Gabriel Mobley had never considered himself a bad man. He had never robbed a bank, never committed some spectacular act of evil that would force him to confront his own reflection with horror. His destruction did not come through one catastrophic mistake. It came through a thousand small choices, a thousand quiet compromises, a thousand moments when he chose what felt good over what was right and convinced himself it did not matter. He lived the kind of life that excused rather than denied and postponed rather than surrendered.

He knew enough about Christianity to be comfortable around it and understood the language. He could bow his head at family dinners, quote a verse, when necessary, nod through a sermon without flinching, but knowing the vocabulary of faith is not the same as living under its authority, and Gabriel preferred a version of belief that required acknowledgment without obedience. He believed in God in theory, but in practice, he lived for the immediate.

Like so many others, Gabriel lived under the illusion that the clock was generous. He assumed tomorrow was guaranteed because yesterday had always arrived. He mistook God's patience for indifference and interpreted the delayed consequence as permanent permission. He believed eternity was something he could address eventually, after he had exhausted the pleasures of the present… he was wrong.

When the world changed, it did not announce itself with a warning tailored to his schedule. It did not pause to accommodate his unfinished intentions. The trumpet sounded, the faithful were taken, and Gabriel remained. The life he had built so casually, revealed itself for what it truly was: a structure raised on sand, impressive in appearance yet fatally unstable.

He sat on the floor of his apartment on the eleventh day after the blackout, the city unnaturally silent, the evidence of whatever had happened lingering in every empty street and abandoned building, but Gabriel was not thinking about the city anymore; his mind had turned inward, toward something far older and far more personal. He was thinking about the Road. Not a physical road carved into asphalt or mapped by street signs, but a spiritual one. The Romans Road.

That was what his grandmother had called it, her voice always soft but certain when she said the name, as though she were introducing him to something sacred and unchanging. It was a path through the book of Romans, she would explain, a sequence of truths laid out by the apostle Paul nearly two thousand years earlier, verses that formed a clear progression from the recognition of sin to the acceptance of salvation, from spiritual death to eternal life. It began with the blunt reality that all have sinned and fallen short of the glory of God, that no one stands righteous on their own merit. It moved to the sobering consequence of that condition, that the wages of sin are death. And then, with deliberate grace, it unfolded into hope: that God demonstrated His love in this, that while we were still sinners Christ died for us; that if you confess with your mouth and believe in your heart that Jesus is Lord, you will be saved. It was not complicated theology. It was a map. A straight line drawn through human failure toward divine mercy.

Gabriel's grandmother had tried to walk him down that road when he was twelve years old. She had sat with him in her small living room, the afternoon light filtering through lace curtains, her worn Bible open to Romans, its margins filled with notes written in careful, looping handwriting. Verse by verse, she had shown him what it meant to be saved. She did not present it as a cultural tradition or a family expectation. She presented it as the truth. As something that mattered more than the distant future, he assumed he would always have.

Gabriel had listened politely. He had nodded at the appropriate moments. When she asked if he understood, he said yes. When she asked if he wanted to pray, he had agreed, because her eyes were bright with hope, and he loved her too much to wound that hope with indifference. So, he repeated the words she guided him through, believing the language forming easily on his young tongue. But he had not meant it, not in the way he was supposed to.

For him, it had been performance. Words shaped to satisfy expectation. The kind of religious participation a child offers to make the adults happy, while fully intending to live however he chooses once he is old enough to make his own decisions. He walked the Romans Road that day in his grandmother's living room, but he never stepped off the curb of his own will. He treated salvation like a ceremony rather than a surrender, and when he left her house that evening, he left the weight of those verses behind with the open Bible on her coffee table, never imagining that one day, in a darkened apartment in a silent city, he would find himself searching for that same road again, only now without the comfort of her guiding voice and without the illusion that there was still plenty of time to decide whether he would follow it.

His grandmother had died of cancer when Gabriel was sixteen. It was quick, the kind that does not negotiate and does not leave room for denial. He had watched it strip weight from her frame and color from her skin, had watched her body weaken while something in her spirit seemed impossibly steady. She faced it with the same simple faith she had tried to pass on to him, praying quietly from her hospital bed, thanking God between waves of pain and speaking about eternity as if it were not an abstract doctrine but a destination she was already preparing to enter. She trusted Him even as her body failed her. At last, she went peacefully, confident in a salvation Gabriel had pretended to accept but had never truly embraced.

At the funeral, he stood beside the casket and felt the strange collision of grief and resentment, because her certainty unsettled him. She had not been afraid. That bothered him more than the cancer itself. She had spoken about heaven as though it were more real than the hospital room, more solid than the IV lines and machines. Gabriel nodded along when relatives spoke about her being "with the Lord," but something in him recoiled. It sounded too neat. Too convenient. Too certain.

Over the next sixteen years, he quietly dismantled everything she had tried to build in him. Not in open rebellion, not with dramatic declarations that he rejected her faith, but through steady indifference. He convinced himself that what she believed had been emotional comfort, nothing more. A coping mechanism for the weak. A story people told themselves to soften the sharp edges of mortality. He told himself that the prayer he had said at twelve had been exactly what it felt like: words. Just syllables arranged to please a dying woman. In doing so, he freed himself, at least that is what he called it.

Then the decline accelerated. What had begun as a subtle compromise hardened into appetite and habit. Alcohol stopped being social and became necessary. Drugs followed, first recreational, then routine, then essential to dull the quiet accusations of his own conscience. Relationships blurred into transactions; women were used for comfort or distraction and discarded when they required something deeper than his surface-level charm. Jobs came and went, lost through negligence, or through the simple arrogance of not showing up and assuming there would always be another opportunity waiting. Bridges burned with family and friends who had grown tired of excuses. His reputation, once respectable, thinned into something people spoke about with lowered voices and resigned expressions.

In truth, he had not merely wandered from faith; he had dismantled it. He stopped praying altogether. He convinced himself that the chaos was temporary; he would get serious later; he would repair the damage eventually. It was the oldest lie a drifting soul tells themselves when destruction is still a form of choice. Those deceptions were comfortable because they removed urgency. They allowed him to continue choosing what was hollow while convincing himself he was choosing what was free.

But the blackout shattered that narrative. The sudden silence of the city stripped away the language he had used to protect himself. No noise to drown out reality. In the quiet, the truth stood unshielded: he had not simply lost the path of faith; he had abandoned it deliberately, mile after mile, until he no longer recognized where it had begun.

If their disappearance meant what he feared it meant, then the faith he had dismissed was not symbolic, and the surrender he had postponed was not optional. The silence forced a single, unavoidable question to the surface: was the Romans Road his grandmother had shown him still open to someone who had spent sixteen years running in the opposite direction? He did not know if the path was still accessible, but for the first time since he was twelve years old, he understood that he had to find out whether a man who had run from God for most of his life could still turn around and run toward Him instead.

Gabriel pushed himself up from the floor and crossed the small living room to his bookshelf. The apartment was dim, lit only by the gray wash of late afternoon filtering through the window, the city outside still unnaturally quiet, as though sound itself had been taken along with the vanished. The shelf held exactly three books. Two were paperbacks he had never finished. The third was his grandmother's bible.

It had been given to him after her funeral, pressed into his hands by an aunt who said she would have wanted him to have it. He had kept it all these years, not out of devotion, but out of guilt. Discarding it would have meant admitting that he had not merely drifted from her faith but rejected it completely. So he had done what was easier. He had placed it on a shelf and allowed dust to settle over it, as though neglect were softer than denial.

He reached for it now and felt the familiar weight of the worn leather cover beneath his fingers, the edges softened by years of use. The leather was cracked along the spine, creased from being opened and reopened. When he lifted it, a faint scent rose from the thin pages, a mixture of paper and time. He ran his thumb along the fore-edge and saw her handwriting before he even opened it, small and steady in the margins, notes written in blue ink, dates carefully inscribed beside certain verses. Some passages were underlined once. Others twice. A few circled completely, as though she had returned to them again and again until they had carved themselves into her heart.

It was not just a book. It was a map she had walked herself. Gabriel did not open it randomly; he actually remembered. The Romans Road began in chapter three, verse twenty-three. She had made him memorize it, had him repeat it until he could recite it without glancing down, until the rhythm of it felt automatic.

He turned the thin pages carefully, the paper almost translucent against the dim light, and found the verse already marked, underlined twice, the date beside it written in her hand from the afternoon she had first walked him through it. He swallowed and read aloud into the stillness of the apartment, his voice sounding unfamiliar in the quiet.

"For all have sinned and fall short of the glory of God."

The words hung in the air. At twelve, the verse had felt abstract. It had described people in the broadest sense, a category that included him but did not confront him. Sin had been a concept then, something discussed in Sunday school and illustrated with simple examples. Falling short had sounded theoretical, like missing a mark he had never clearly seen.

At thirty-two, after sixteen years of proving the verse personally, it no longer felt abstract. It felt accusatory. The word all did not blur him into a crowd; it isolated him, his choices, and lifestyle. addictions.

The verse simply stated a fact, and in that simplicity, it became a mirror. Gabriel did not have to search for examples. He had lived them.

The Romans Road did not begin with comfort. It began with recognition and the stripping away of illusion. His grandmother had told him that you cannot understand salvation until you understand why you need it. That the road does not start with grace; it starts with truth.

Gabriel knew with a clarity that his sixteen years had not been accidental stumbles but active choices. He had not merely drifted an inch below God's standard; he had stepped away from it deliberately, repeatedly, confidently.

Falling short of God's glory meant falling short of His perfection. It meant missing a mark that was not flexible, not adjustable to suit culture or preference. Gabriel had not just fallen short, but he had crashed and burned beneath it. He had proven comprehensively that he was nowhere near the glory of God.

When the trumpet sounded and the surrendered were taken, Gabriel had remained. Anchored to the earth by his own will. By sixteen years of postponing repentance as though it were an appointment he could reschedule indefinitely.

He turned and really looked at the room for the first time. Trash overflowed from a bin he had stopped bothering to empty. Clothes were piled in corners; the coffee table was sticky with dried alcohol. Bottles lay on their sides where he had dropped them days earlier. The air carried the stale scent of neglect.

It was not just a mess but evidence. The physical manifestation of an internal condition he had refused to acknowledge. Disorder outside mirrors disorder within. A life of sin eventually produces a life of chaos.

The truth was simpler and harder. It was never too late while you were still breathing. While your heart still beats. While your mind still had the capacity to recognize truth and respond to it. If he could still read Romans, if he could still feel conviction pressing against his chest, then the door was not yet closed.

The Romans Road had not vanished when the world changed. It was still there, ink pressed into thin pages, mapped out the same way it had been for two thousand years, offering the same progression from death to life. The first step was acknowledgment, 2nd consequence, 3rd provision, and 4th response. It was not mystical but clear.

Gabriel could still walk it if he stopped performing and started surrendering. He sank back into the chair, his fingers still tracing the worn edges of the Bible, and read the next verse his grandmother had made him memorize so many years ago. Romans chapter six, verse twenty-three.

"For the wages of sin are death, but the gift of God is eternal life in Christ Jesus, our Lord."

The word wages struck him now with a force that had been absent at twelve. Wages are the payment due for work performed. Gabriel had been working at sin for sixteen years, deliberately pursuing it as if mastery of vice could somehow satisfy a deeper longing he had never named.

Gabriel felt it all in that moment, the fullness of what he had earned. Every lie told, every promise broken, every bridge burned. Every moment, he had chosen immediate gratification over eternal truth. All the energy spent shaping himself into a man who could ignore God, all the clever rationalizations, all the performance of belief without surrender. It had not gone unnoticed.

He had earned nothing good. Not redemption. Not honor. Not love. Not peace. Not even safety from the consequences of his own choices. The life he had built with his own hands, the years he had treated as free, the faith he had postponed and dismissed, they had accumulated into nothing but death. The undeniable truth was that sixteen years of running from God had resulted in nothing but emptiness, and Gabriel knew, with a painful clarity, that if he did not walk that path now, he might never have another chance.

It did not end with the stark declaration that the wages of sin are death. There was a contrast, a *but*. That word carried the weight of possibility, of hope, of an entirely different reality.

"But the gift of God is eternal life."

The words sank into him differently at thirty-two than they had at twelve. Life was not earned. It could not be purchased with good works or careful obedience. It was offered and extended freely, without condition. Only Jesus could transform the death Gabriel had earned through sixteen years of active rebellion into life that could not be earned by any effort, no matter how sincere.

He read the verses again, letting them settle deep in his mind, like sunlight penetrating a darkened room. He had worked diligently at sin, accumulating failures with an almost methodical efficiency. He had pursued every indulgence, every selfish desire, every easy pleasure that promised temporary satisfaction and permanent distance from God. He had built a life around his own choices, and in doing so, he had earned nothing but death. And yet, in the same breath, the Scripture offered something he could not earn, something he did not deserve, something that transcended the ledger of his failures entirely: a gift. Not conditional, corrected mistakes, or proven worth. A gift freely extended to anyone willing to receive it, even someone like him, someone whose life was a record of defiance and disregard.

The distinction hit him with a force he could not ignore. Wages were earned, but grace was given. Gabriel realized with a painful clarity that he qualified for grace precisely because he qualified for nothing else. His own accomplishments, striving, and attempts to master life had produced only separation and decay.

He turned to the next verse on the Romans Road, carefully marked in his grandmother's handwriting, a guide left for him decades earlier. Romans chapter five, verse eight:

"But God demonstrates His own love toward us, in that while we were still sinners, Christ died for us."

The simplicity of it was devastating in its precision. Christ did not wait for Gabriel to clean up. Christ died for Gabriel while he was still a sinner, and also while he was still actively running in the opposite direction.

It was past tense, something already accomplished. Not contingent on future obedience. Not conditional on proof of worth, but complete. The payment had been made, the gift had been extended, while Gabriel was still steeped in sin, still in the process of earning the death that he knew he deserved. The Romans Road did not begin with perfection. It began with acknowledgment. It began with recognition that life as he had known it was.

The road was still open, and the gift was still being offered. Gabriel could still walk it if he chose and truly meant it this time. If he stopped performing faith and began surrendering to it.

Gabriel felt something deep inside him give way, the hard self-fashioned barrier that had kept God at arm's length finally cracking. It wasn't the result of some external force or a moment of dramatic revelation. It was recognition. The illusion of control he had clung to for sixteen years, the carefully constructed shell that allowed him to live in rebellion while pretending he was steering his own life, was splintering under the weight of a truth he had long denied: God loved him.

Not some abstract version of him, not the boy who had repeated memorized verses without meaning them, but God loved Gabriel Mobley, the same man who had spent sixteen years actively rejecting that love. God loved him despite every excuse and every moment of defiance.

He realized the reason the Romans Road still existed, the reason the path his grandmother had tried to show him remained accessible. God had kept it open and extended the gift even when Gabriel had stubbornly chosen the wages. God had loved him while he continued to accumulate debt, while he continued to walk in darkness.

He hadn't cried in years, trained himself not to feel too deeply, but the tears came anyway, breaking through sixteen years of suppression. They ran down his face with no apology and the realization that God loved him.

Gabriel's hands lingered on the thin pages of the Bible as he turned to the next verse, the worn leather spine creaking softly in the quiet of the apartment. Romans chapter ten, verse nine, stared back at him from the page.

"That if you confess with your mouth the Lord Jesus, and believe in your heart that God has raised Him from the dead, you will be saved."

The simplicity of it struck him. The path of salvation did not require elaborate rituals, complicated theology, or heroic effort. It required only two things: confession and belief. Speakit aloud and trust in it. Acknowledge Jesus as Lord, that God had raised Him from the dead, and you will be saved.

He repeated the words softly, almost a whisper, *"Confess. Believe, and you will be saved."* The syllables felt strange on his tongue at first, foreign after years of rejection and defiance, yet as he spoke them, they began to settle, like stepping stones underfoot in a darkened room. Something inside Gabriel shifted as he realized that the first step of the Romans Road was no longer abstract; it was real, present, and it was waiting for him to walk it.

Gabriel's hands trembled slightly as he clutched the Bible, but he did not release it. Now, for the first time, he could confess with his mouth and surrender with his heart, allowing the words to leave his lips while the conviction rooted itself deep inside. The verse had not just instructed thought or private reflection. It demanded a declaration. Confession was not a silent arrangement between him and God. It was spoken, given voice, made audible to the empty apartment, to the silence outside, to the God who had never stopped watching.

He spoke, voice shaking but gaining strength with each repetition, "Jesus is Lord." Not just a good teacher, not a figure from history to admire at a distance, but Lord and Master. The One with power over everything, including the one thing Gabriel had claimed ownership of for sixteen years: his own life. For sixteen years, he had behaved as though he alone ruled, as though his will, his desires, his timing mattered more than the eternal order he had mocked. But no longer.

"I am done," he whispered, voice growing firmer, more resolute. "I'm done pretending I'm in control. I'm done acting as I know better. Jesus is Lord, of everything, everyone, and… me."

The confession began to feel right. Freeing in ways he had never imagined. Saying it aloud was not just about words, but about giving up the throne he had held so stubbornly for sixteen years, and in that admission, he discovered an unexpected relief.

He continued, the words gathering momentum, shaping themselves into a prayer that was both declaration and surrender, "I believe God raised Jesus from the dead. Not just as a historical fact, but as a present reality. I believe death is not final. I believe resurrection is real. I believe God has power over the grave."

Something that had been dead for sixteen years began to stir, alive for the first time, breathing the gift of life he had finally chosen to receive.

The Romans Road did not end with confession and belief; it led to salvation. Where restitution was possible. To a life that reflected surrender rather than merely claiming it. The road did not conclude at the moment of prayer; it opened into a different direction entirely.

Gabriel moved to the small desk tucked against the wall, clearing aside an empty bottle and a stack of unopened mail. He pulled open the drawer and found paper and a pen, the simple, ordinary tools of permanence. Speaking had mattered. Confession had mattered. But writing would anchor it. Writing would make it concrete. Not just words released into the air and swallowed by silence, but words fixed in ink. He sat down and began,

Romans 5:8 — God demonstrates His love toward us in that while we were still sinners, Christ died for us.

He paused, then continued beneath it in his own handwriting,

While I was still sinning, still wrecking my life… Christ died for me.

He stared at the sentence for a long moment, reflecting an unconditional love. Love that acted while he was still accumulating debt. Love that did not wait to be proven.

The journey had begun, but begun was the operative word. Salvation, he now understood, was instantaneous. The moment he genuinely believed, genuinely surrendered, something had shifted eternally. But transformation was not instantaneous; it was a process. Being saved did not mean being perfected. It did not mean the old habits evaporated or the consequences disappeared. It meant the foundation had changed.

Now came the daily following, the repeated choice to build on this new foundation rather than drift back toward the old one. The steady, persistent surrender that would keep tonight's confession from becoming just another emotional moment that faded into routine.

He thought about the idea of daily reckoning, about the discipline of examining the day. He would need that. Sixteen years of patterns did not dissolve because of one prayer, no matter how sincere. Sixteen years of choosing sin had carved pathways into his mind and habits into his life that would attempt to reassert themselves the moment vigilance relaxed. The pull would come. The old voice would whisper that nothing had really changed.

Gabriel understood the difference now. He knew he was saved, but being saved did not remove responsibility; it clarified it. It meant learning to live as someone who belonged to a different Lord. It meant aligning his actions with the confession he had spoken. Rebuilding what he had broken where possible.

Gabriel placed the pen down and exhaled slowly. The road had not ended in that chair; it had just begun. And for the first time in sixteen years, he was not running from it.

Then his thoughts turned outward, toward the wreckage that had names attached to it. The relationships he had fractured. The people he had wounded through sixteen years of selfishness disguised as independence. His parents, who had watched him drift and had exhausted themselves trying to pull him back. It was a long list. Longer than he would like to admit.

He knew he could not rewind time or erase memory. He could not undo the damage of sixteen years or restore every bridge he had burned. Some people might never answer his call. Some losses might remain permanent, but you could take responsibility instead of hiding behind excuses. Salvation did not erase consequences, but it changed how he faced them. He would apologize where he could. He would repay what he had taken. He would confess wrong without defending himself. It would not redeem the past, but it would honor the God who had redeemed him.

The Romans Road had led him from death to life, and if he was living that life starting now, then it had to show itself in action as well as confession. The direction had changed. The Lord of his life had changed, which means his choices would also have to change.

The day moved quietly around him as the light shifted from gray to gold and then slowly dimmed again. Gabriel began to clean; he gathered trash into bags and washed sticky surfaces. He opened windows to let fresh air push back the stale smell of alcohol. Each small act felt less like self-improvement and more like alignment, as though his external space were slowly reflecting an internal shift.

When the room was finally still again, cleaner than it had been in years, he sat on the floor with his back against the couch and bowed his head. There were no elaborate words left, just simplicity.

"Lord Jesus. Only You."

It was the truth that would sustain him when emotion faded, and discipline was tested. Jesus had saved him, and it was only he who mattered when everything else was stripped away, when illusions collapsed, and when the world itself fell silent.

Gabriel opened his grandmother's Bible one more time, his fingers moving with intention now rather than hesitation. He did not turn back to the Romans Road, but instead to the end of Romans, to a passage he remembered seeing underlined again and again in her careful handwriting. Chapter eight, verses thirty-eight and thirty-nine. The ink in the margins was darker there, layered over itself from multiple readings. These were not decorative underlines; they were anchors. He drew in a slow breath and read aloud, his voice no longer trembling but grounded.

"For I am persuaded, that neither death, nor life, nor angels, nor principalities, nor powers, nor things present, nor things to come, nor height, nor depth, nor any other created thing, shall be able to separate us from the love of God, which is in Christ Jesus our Lord."

The words filled the room, pressing against the silence that had defined the last eleven days. Nothing can separate us, not death, angels, or demons. Not present circumstances or future uncertainty. Not height or depth or anything in all of creation. Nothing, absolutely nothing, can separate us from the love of God in Christ Jesus.

Gabriel lowered the Bible slightly, letting the magnitude of that promise settle over him. For sixteen years, he had attempted separation. He had run from God's love and rejected it. Drowned it out with noise. He built walls high and thick, convinced that if he distanced himself far enough, long enough, he could live untouched by it. He had pursued sin not only because he wanted pleasure, but because he wanted silence, silence from the persistent echo of his grandmother's faith.

Yet, the verse did say nothing will separate, but that nothing can. Separation was not an achievement available to him. It was not something he could successfully manufacture through rebellion or neglect. The love of God in Christ Jesus was stronger than his attempts to reject it, deeper than his accumulated sin, and more persistent than his resistance.

In that moment, he stopped running and walked the Romans Road toward surrender instead of away from it; he discovered what his grandmother had always known. What she had clung to in hospital rooms and whispered through pain.

Gabriel chose differently, and the moment he walked back toward God, he discovered that God had never moved, had never created the distance he had felt so deeply for sixteen years. The separation had not been initiated by heaven. It had not been sustained by divine silence. God had been waiting, offering love, extending grace, keeping the Romans Road open for whenever Gabriel was finally ready to walk it.

Gabriel closed the Bible and set it carefully on the clean table, his movements steady now, intentional rather than uncertain. The worn leather rested beneath his palm for a moment before he let it go, as though he were acknowledging the weight of what it had carried him through. And if God could do that, if God could save someone like Gabriel, someone who had spent sixteen years actively choosing against Him, then God could do anything. If He could transform wages of death into the gift of life, He could take confession and create salvation. He could sustain Gabriel through whatever tomorrow would bring.

Only Jesus had saved him; He would sustain him, and it is only He who matters when everything else fails. Gabriel spoke into the darkness, not to himself but to God. His prayer was not constructed with care to sound impressive. It was gratitude, simple and direct.

"Thank you for keeping the road open. Thank you for waiting while I ran. Thank You for loving me while I still sinned. For the gift I did not earn while I was accumulating wages, I did earn. Thank you to my grandmother, who showed me the path even when I was not ready to walk it. Thank you for preserving her Bible, and for bringing me back to it. Thank You for saving me, not through my effort, but through Your grace. Not through my works, but through faith. Thank You, Jesus, for being sufficient when I was not.

The prayer was everything his prayers had not been during sixteen years of running. It was honest. was free of bargaining and performance. It was the prayer of someone who had stopped resisting and started trusting. He was no longer trying to earn what had already been given. He was no longer trying to negotiate what had already been settled at the cross.

Tomorrow would come with its challenges, its temptations, its old patterns trying to reassert themselves, its former life attempting to reclaim what had been surrendered. The habits of sixteen years would not disappear in a single evening. But tonight, Gabriel was grateful simply to be alive.

He felt hope. Not wishful thinking that denies circumstances, but genuine hope rooted in genuine faith, rooted in genuine salvation. Hope anchored not in his strength, but in Christ's sufficiency. The path forward was clearer than the path behind. Behind him were years of striving, resisting, and running. Before him was grace, and a life no longer defined by separation, but by nearness.

"Lord Jesus, only You. Thank you… Thank you for bringing me home." The prayer did not feel dramatic. It did not feel theatrical or heightened. It felt settled. True in a way that did not need volume to validate it. The words moved into the darkness and remained there, not echoing back in doubt, but resting in assurance. It was a declaration, but more than anything, it was the language of arrival. The language of someone who had been wandering so long he had forgotten what stillness felt like.

Gabriel stood at the window and looked out into the quiet night. The world outside remained unchanged; nothing in the visible landscape reflected the magnitude of what had shifted inside him. Yet everything had shifted. He was no longer orienting his life around himself, no longer defining freedom as autonomy; the axis had moved. The center had changed, and it was now Jesus.

He prayed again, the words no longer rushed but understood. "Thank you for your grace and for bringing me home."

Grace given while he was still sinning, and while he was still running. Grace that did not weaken with rejection or expire with delay. For sixteen years, he had assumed that distance meant disqualification. He had believed that enough rebellion would eventually close the door. But the door had not closed, and the road had not collapsed.

The Romans Road had led exactly where it promised it would lead… home. It led to Jesus, to sufficiency that did not fluctuate with performance. To love that did not retreat when challenged. To salvation that did not depend on his ability to maintain it.

This was the sound of "Only." Not minimalism or reduction, but clarity. Only Jesus saves, only Jesus is enough when everything else is stripped away, only He remains when emotion fades, and discipline wavers and circumstances shift. Only Jesus carries the weight of eternity without strain.

Three days passed, and in those three days, Gabriel learned that salvation was not merely a moment to remember but a life to inhabit. The initial surge of relief and gratitude settled into something steadier and deeper, like a river finding its banks after a storm. Each morning, he rose with intention, not out of fear of losing what he had received, but out of desire to live consistently with it. He practiced daily reckoning, examining his thoughts and motives in the quiet light before dawn. When pride surfaced, he named it. When temptation whispered, he answered it with truth rather than impulse. He prayed not with desperation now, but with dependence. He was discovering that surrender was not a single act but a continuous posture.

He began making amends where it was possible. Some conversations were halting and awkward, shaped by years of distance that could not be erased in a single apology. Some messages were met with silence. Others were answered with guarded grace. He did not control the outcomes; he only controlled his obedience. He repaid what he had taken. He admitted wrong without qualification. He listened to pain without defending himself. In each step, he felt the foundation beneath him holding firm, not because he had suddenly become righteous, but because he was building on only

Jesus instead of on himself. The Romans Road had not led him to a private emotional experience; it had led him into a transformed direction of living.

On the fourteenth morning after the blackout, Gabriel awakened to a sound unlike anything he had ever heard. It was a trumpet, but it bore no resemblance to the earlier blast that had shattered the world two weeks before. That first trumpet had carried terror and separation; it had divided families and emptied cities. This sound was different in tone and texture. It was not shrill, yet it was absolute. It did not assault the ears, yet it commanded the soul. The note seemed to exist everywhere at once, resonating through walls, through pavement, through the air itself. It vibrated in his chest and along his spine, as though the architecture of his body recognized its authority.

Gabriel sat upright in bed as the sound continued, sustained and sovereign. The room around him felt charged with presence. Sunlight filtered faintly through the curtains, but it was already being overtaken by something brighter, something not native to Earth. He moved to the window, drawn by instinct more than thought, and as he looked out over the city, he saw the sky begin to change.

The heavens were opening.

This was no metaphor, no poetic imagination crafted to comfort the fearful. The expanse above the skyline seemed to part, as though an unseen veil were being drawn back by hands of immeasurable strength. The blue of morning fractured into radiant brilliance, and light poured through the widening breach in waves that were not merely luminous but alive. It was light with depth and dimension, light that seemed to carry intelligence and holiness within it. The air shimmered, and the ordinary outline of buildings and streets took on a fragile quality, as though they were sketches about to be replaced by a greater reality.

Within that descending glory, Gabriel saw movement. Figures were rising from every direction. From apartment balconies and hospital rooms, from sidewalks and open fields, from places of worship and places of quiet solitude, men and women were being lifted upward. They were not struggling; they were not striving. They were being gathered. Mortality was giving way to immortality before his eyes. What had been bound to gravity was now responding to a higher call.

As he watched, Gabriel felt something within him respond. It was not a physical tug at first, but a summons in his spirit that was unmistakable. The trumpet's call seemed to translate itself into meaning inside him, and though no audible words were formed, he understood it clearly: "Come home."

The invitation was personal. It was not addressed to the masses alone; it was addressed to him.

A warmth spread through his body, not heat that burned but vitality that transformed. The heaviness he had always associated with physical existence began to loosen. His limbs felt lighter, his breath deeper, as though every cell were being restructured by unseen hands. He did not feel himself dying; he felt himself becoming. The mortal was clothing itself in immortality. The corruptible was putting on incorruption. Time's claim on him was dissolving.

His feet lifted from the floor without effort. He rose slowly at first, the room receding beneath him. He passed through the ceiling and roof as though solid matter had become permeable in the presence of divine authority. The cool morning air enveloped him, but even that sensation felt secondary to the overwhelming awareness of being called. Around him, countless others were ascending as well, their faces illuminated by the same radiance that poured from the opened heavens. Some wept with joy. Some laughed in astonishment. All were drawn upward by the same irresistible grace.

As the city shrank below him, Gabriel understood with crystalline clarity why he was among them. It was not because three days of obedience had erased sixteen years of rebellion. It was not because he had managed to correct enough of his past to qualify for glory. It was because he had confessed Jesus as Lord. It was because he had believed that God raised Him from the dead. It was because he had accepted the gift rather than clinging to wages. The Romans Road had not been a formula; it had been a path, and he had walked it. Grace had done what effort never could.

The light grew brighter as he ascended, yet it did not blind him. Instead, it clarified everything. The horizon of earth faded into softness while the horizon of eternity sharpened into breathtaking reality. The open sky was no longer simply an expanse of brilliance; it was a threshold. Beyond it stretched a realm of color and depth beyond earthly vocabulary, a landscape alive with glory. The atmosphere itself seemed to pulse with praise, though no single voice could be distinguished. It was as though creation had reached its intended crescendo.

Then Gabriel Jesus stood at the center of the unfolding glory, radiant with a majesty that was both overwhelming and intimate. His presence carried the weight of sovereignty and the warmth of compassion in perfect harmony. There was no distance in His gaze, no cold detachment of judgment. There was recognition, delight, and welcome. The scars in His hands were visible, not as wounds, but as trophies of redemption. The light that surrounded Him did not obscure His face; it revealed it.

As Gabriel drew nearer, he heard the voice that had called him through the trumpet, now clear and resonant, rich with authority and tenderness.

"Welcome home, beloved. You are redeemed by My grace, sustained by My faithfulness, and received by My love."

The words entered him not as sound alone but as fulfillment. Every fear he had once harbored about rejection dissolved in that moment. Every lingering doubt about belonging vanished. He was not arriving as a tolerated guest; he was arriving as a welcomed son.

Gabriel crossed the threshold from earth into glory, and the transformation completed itself. What had begun in confession reached its consummation in presence. He was no longer walking by faith; he was seeing face to face. The one he had trusted in the quiet of his apartment now stood before him in unveiled splendor. The journey that had begun with "Lord Jesus, only You" culminated in the reality of Jesus before him.

As he entered into that glory, surrounded by the redeemed and enveloped in unending light, his final earthly prayer rose naturally and completely.

"Lord Jesus, only You. Thank You for the Romans Road. Thank you for the grace. Thank you for bringing me home. Only You have saved me. Only You have sustained me. Only You are enough for eternity."

Home was not streets of gold alone, though beauty surpassed imagination. Home was not merely the absence of sorrow, though sorrow had no place there. Home was Jesus Himself. The One who had loved him while he was still sinning. The One who had kept the road open while he ran. The One who had been sufficient for thirty-two years of ignorance and three days of obedience alike.

The trumpet's call faded into eternal praise. The separation between heaven and earth was no more. The Romans Road had led exactly where it promised it would lead: not to religion, not to self-improvement, but to communion. To glory. To only Jesus.

And in that everlasting presence, Gabriel knew with unshakable certainty that the sound of "Only" had become the sound of "Always." Forever in the presence of Jesus, who is sufficient, who is enough, and reigns without end. Amen!